Praise for
Unbottled Potential

"Amanda is a compassionate and innovative thought leader
in the world of personal development and alcohol-free living.
She's also a powerful teacher who can help you step
into your truest potential."

—**Kris Carr**, *New York Times* **bestselling author
and wellness leader**

"Amanda Kuda makes a convincing case for choosing
sobriety as the key to us realizing our full potential. Her book
is packed with 'aha' moments and concrete takeaways that
will get you excited to test her theory for yourself."

—**Ruby Warrington, author of** *Sober Curious,*
The Sober Curious Reset, **and** *Women Without Kids*

"*Unbottled Potential* is a beacon of hope, providing practical
advice, empowering exercises, and real-life success stories
that will inspire and motivate you to live your best life.
A truly transformative read!"

—**Jen Gottlieb, cofounder of Super Connector Media
and author of** *Be Seen*

"Amanda is trailblazing a path for women choosing to
live an alcohol-free life. Watch out, world, she is
gonna wake you up."

—**Jessica Zweig, author of** *Be.*

"With remarkable insight and authenticity, Amanda offers
invaluable wisdom and guidance for anyone seeking to
unlock their true potential and embrace a life filled with
clarity, vitality, and limitless possibilities."

—**Sabrina Soto, designer, TV host, and author of**
Sabrina Soto Home Design

unbottled POTENTIAL

BREAK UP WITH ALCOHOL

——————————— AND ———————————

BREAK THROUGH TO YOUR BEST LIFE

Amanda Kuda

AVERY

an imprint of Penguin Random House

New York

AVERY

an imprint of Penguin Random House LLC
penguinrandomhouse.com

Illustrations on page 94 by Amanda Sheeren, Okay, Yeah! Design

Most Avery books are available at special quantity discounts for bulk purchase
for sales promotions, premiums, fundraising, and educational needs. Special
books or book excerpts also can be created to fit specific needs. For details, write
SpecialMarkets@penguinrandomhouse.com.

Library of Congress Cataloging-in-Publication Data

Names: Kuda, Amanda, author.
Title: Unbottled potential: break up with alcohol and break through
   to your best life / Amanda Kuda.
Description: New York: Avery, [2023] | Includes bibliographical references.
Identifiers: LCCN 2023005645 (print) | LCCN 2023005646 (ebook) |
ISBN 9780593538678 (trade paperback) | ISBN 9780593538685 (epub)
Subjects: LCSH: Temperance. | Drinking of alcoholic beverages. |
   Alcoholism. | Self-realization.
Classification: LCC HV5060.K83 2023 (print) | LCC HV5060 (ebook) |
   DDC 362.292—dc23/eng/20230626
LC record available at https://lccn.loc.gov/2023005645
LC ebook record available at https://lccn.loc.gov/2023005646

Printed in the United States of America
1st Printing

Book design by Shannon Nicole Plunkett

For Monroe, the sweetest white ball of fluff there ever was. Thank you for teaching me the power of unconditional, reciprocal love. Your presence during my writing was deeply missed. I know you left this world to make room for this book, and so much more.

Contents

Introduction

I woke up on New Year's Eve (not New Year's Day, mind you, *New Year's Eve*) of 2016 with a ferocious hangover. The night before, I'd planned to go out and have just a few drinks. As often happened, my plans were thwarted, and I ended up having a few too many.

I played back the scene in my head. I should have gone home after dinner. Instead, I was persuaded to go barhopping and dancing downtown. I love dancing. I remember bopping around joyfully to 2000s hip-hop and guzzling a novelty spiked drink served in a children's juice pouch.

The next morning, I dragged myself from bed and called an Uber to take me back to my vehicle, which was still parked safely at a restaurant it was never intended to stay at. My stomach turned in the stuffy car. From the rearview mirror dangled a sinfully pungent air freshener, clearly intended to camouflage the car's musty odor. The combination was nearly the undoing of me.

Back in my own car, I gasped for fresh air as I sat there unsteadily. I tried to settle myself as I wondered if I was doomed to vomit in a restaurant parking lot as innocent families were making their way in for brunch. I immediately canceled my brunch plans with friends, lacking both the willpower and the stomach to socialize. I spent most of New Year's Eve day wallowing on the sofa, wondering if this—an endless string of happy hours, hangovers, boozy brunches, and Sunday Fundays—was all there was to life.

The vibrant social life I was living had once seemed so glamorous. From this particular vantage point, my social obligations felt more like a burden. For the life of me, I couldn't understand where I'd gone wrong.

From the outside, it certainly looked like I was living the good life. I was a young, healthy, single, attractive woman with a thriving career and active social life. I had spent the better part of the last decade building my lifestyle to be exactly what it was: a shallow, repetitive merry-go-round of ladder climbing and elbow rubbing that was sold to me as "the dream." Surely, to someone else this was a dream; I should be satisfied, right? Yet as I sat there, nearly catatonic on my sofa, too hung over to think clearly, I realized I was, in fact, living some sadistic, self-imposed nightmare.

When I took a good look at the life I'd built for myself, it wasn't difficult to see that most of my friendships lacked depth, my romantic life was unfulfilling, I was working myself ragged punching the clock for someone else's dream, and my life was void of the spiritual connection that I desperately desired.

As I sat there, disillusioned by it all, I asked myself a question I'd been pondering for months: Would everything be better if I just stopped drinking? It seemed almost silly. How could one small decision like abstaining from alcohol make everything better? Yet I knew in my soul that I was meant for something big and important in this lifetime. I'd actually known this since I was a little girl. I believed that enriching friendships and true love were possible, even though I hadn't fully experienced them. I sensed that joy and happiness were available to me, although I'd spent almost ten years trying to figure out if something was wrong with me. I knew that abundance and fulfilling work were not mutually exclusive, and at this point, I had neither. On one hand, my desires felt so familiar, and on the other, they all seemed slightly out of reach. I wondered again if maybe, just maybe, alcohol was the thing holding me back.

There was only one problem: I didn't have a problem. I asked myself multiple times if I was powerless over alcohol. Each time, the answer was a resounding no. I wasn't in denial. I was, in fact, nothing more than a normal (albeit heavy at times) social drinker. As I looked around, it was clear that there was nothing abnormal about my drinking habits. Every other young, social woman was drinking just as much as, if not more than, I was. So, no, I didn't have a problem, but in that miserable moment lying on my sofa, I decided I was curious enough to explore what life could be like without the hazy veil of alcohol clouding it.

I began my journey with an intentional thirty-day break and extended that break to ninety days, then six months, then a full year. As I abstained, I also committed to investing the time and money I once spent on partying on my own personal, emotional, and spiritual development. Quite unexpectedly, I came to a place where alcohol was no longer good or bad, right or wrong. Alcohol became an option that merely existed. From this perspective, it also became an option that I was no longer interested in. Through my journey, I stopped thinking about drinking entirely. The result was not instantaneous. Nonetheless, it was miraculous. After months of abstaining, praying, meditating, journaling, and studying, I began to understand alcohol, and myself, differently. From this place, alcohol seemed completely insignificant.

My new realization about drinking was this: alcohol is our socially acceptable solution—a cure-all for ailments large and small. We consume alcohol with the hope of subtly shifting our disposition or elevating and exaggerating an existing personality trait. Yet the persona we create with alcohol is false. The more I looked closely at my relationship with drinking, the more I realized alcohol was the root of a system of other behaviors, habits, and beliefs I was using to keep myself small.

Unwittingly, I used alcohol to dull my brightness and dilute my potential. Alcohol kept me safely tethered to the ground, where I continued marching in unison with everyone else. But I was not meant to be tethered tightly to the ground; I was meant to soar. I believe you, too, are meant to soar.

I know the possibility that is available to you, and—even though we may not have met—I want that for you so badly. I want you to experience joy and happiness and bliss and success beyond your wildest dreams. I want you to realize your fullest potential, live as your most authentic self, and connect to your soul. If you are even the tiniest bit curious about what life could be like without alcohol, keep reading. This book is for you.

Come with me as I guide you through a discovery of just how wrong we've gotten it when it comes to alcohol. I'll guide you to become aware of all the ways we've allowed alcohol to invade our lives, stifling our birthright to be fully self-expressed. When we allow alcohol to enter our lives in this way, we lower our sense of self-worth and block our ability to self-actualize, achieve, and connect to our internal wisdom. Deep down, we each crave this type of life, but we get lost in our pursuit. We end up doing ordinary things yet expecting extraordinary results.

Drinking becomes both a symptom and a self-prescribed treatment. We imbibe to fit in and play safely within the bounds society has constructed for us. We drink again to numb our dissatisfaction with the mediocre life we've built.

Throughout my twenties, I played out the story that drinking was normal and "cool." I drank to hide my insecurities and reveal my outgoing side. I drank to cover up the fact that I'd lost touch with my authentic self and built myself into a lifestyle I was incredibly discontented with. It was a vicious cycle, and I saw no easy way out. Perhaps you've been there, too.

When we allow our potential to be bottled up in the drinking culture, we fail to achieve the emotional depth, personal success, professional excellence, relational fulfillment, and spiritual connection that are available to us. Rather, we settle for what appears to be "good enough." If you're reading this now, I hope you're over and done with settling for mediocrity. I hope you're ready to live a life that, up until now, you've only dreamed of.

If so, I'm here to guide you through the most common stumbling blocks we all face while trying to find freedom from alcohol in a world that seems to be—okay, *is*—obsessed with booze. I'll give you the insight and tools you need to bravely explore your relationship with alcohol and help you learn what life can be like if you choose to unbottle your potential.

Whether you're looking to break up with booze or just want to find a less-frequent, less-volatile relationship with alcohol, the concepts I outline in this book will serve as a solid foundation for renegotiating the way you feel about drinking.

It is my greatest honor to serve you in any way as you work to unbottle your potential. I am both a curious student and a willing teacher on this path. My understanding of our relationship with alcohol is rooted in psychology, personal development, and spiritual study. As such, I know some of the concepts I introduce to you may be challenging or even triggering. I ask that you keep going and read with an open mind. What follows in the pages of this book is a vision of what life could be like for you. Welcome to *Unbottled Potential*.

part one

BOTTLED-UP BRILLIANCE

CHAPTER 1

You Don't Need to Have a Problem

Getting Over the Social Stigma around Sobriety

It's 2016, and I'm just a few months into my thirties when I find myself staring at a Google search bar. My fingers hover tentatively over the keyboard, preparing to take one of the many quizzes designed to help you determine if you have a problem with alcohol. I answer the questions one by one and wait for the results to appear on my screen. When they do, I let out a huge sigh of relief. The quiz confirms what I had already suspected: my name is Amanda, and I'm *not* an alcoholic.

Even though this was the anticipated outcome, I furrow my brow in confusion. If I'm not an alcoholic, why do I have this nagging feeling that I should quit drinking? It's perplexing because, as far as I know, people who don't have a problem with alcohol don't just quit drinking . . . do they? Further, how did I, an average, run-of-the-mill social drinker, end up here, pondering what it would be like to pursue a life of sobriety at the ripe age of thirty? I feel like a weirdo for even considering it.

Breaking up with booze doesn't make sense. I have no real reason to question my relationship with alcohol . . . it is by no means ruining my life. In fact, from the outside looking in, my life looks pretty rad. I have a great job, a cute apartment, and a nice car; I'm physically fit and I have an active social schedule. Yet I can't shake the feeling that alcohol has outworn its welcome in my life.

When I take a serious look at my drinking, I conclude that my relationship with alcohol has been rather unremarkable. There have been no rock bottoms or ruined relationships. I haven't caused myself physical harm or put my job in jeopardy. I'm not drinking alone, neglecting my responsibilities, or fitting any of the stereotypes they tell you to look for in problem drinkers. I'm also not drinking any more than my peers, who, by the way, also appear to be kicking ass at life. Although I go out frequently, my drinking has not led me down the path of drugs. Alcohol is my one vice, and a socially acceptable one at that.

I've been able to confirm time and time again that my drinking is normal. I've even gone so far as to ask my therapist if she thinks I should quit. I'm met with a quizzical stare; it's clear that she hasn't been given the tools to confront sobriety outside the bounds of addiction. She suggests I simply try to be more mindful with moderation.

Try as I might, mindfulness and moderation don't seem to stick, and I can't escape the growing curiosity about what my world could look like without the happy hours, boozy brunches, Sunday Fundays, and crippling hangovers. I cannot, no matter how intently I try, ignore the instinctual knowing that alcohol is holding me back from living up to my truest potential.

However, this is precisely what I've been trying to do ever since the feeling began to surface: Stifle it. Ignore it. Forget about it. On one hand, I know my life would be better without alcohol. On the other, I'm afraid of what my life would look like if I chose to defy the one social norm that I've built so much of my persona around. In my world, drinking alcohol is synonymous with being fun, cool, sexy, relaxed, and sophisticated. Until recently, I'd never once questioned the place alcohol had in my life because I never *needed* to. Rather, I coveted alcohol as a required social lubricant, a welcome form of liquid courage, an elixir to enhance my mood, and a potion to drown my sorrows. In fact, my newfound sober curiosity is borderline annoying. Am I determined to be absolutely no fun? Am I some sort of weird recluse trying to finagle my way into a life of certain solitude and social rejection? Am I trying to render myself undatable? I'm only thirty; isn't this supposed to be fun?

The fact of the matter is, drinking *was* fun, or at least I thought it was. It was fun until I started feeling like complete shit for days, no matter how much or little I drank. It was fun until my hangovers started showing up with an unwelcome case of anxiety. It was fun until it felt like never-ending commitments to networking events and social outings were my certain future. In other words, it was fun until it wasn't.

The solution seems obvious enough: quit drinking. But if you've grappled with these same feelings, you know the solution is simple; it's just not that easy in a world where alcohol is the answer for both celebration and commiseration. It's not that easy in a society where alcohol is the consummate cure-all for everything from minor discomfort to massive heartbreak. It's not that easy when your social life is structured around drinking and you're frankly not sure how to navigate a normal life without the glue that seems to hold everything together.

Determined to find a better way, I returned to my laptop and began typing the next most logical search phrase I could think of: "How to quit drinking if you're not an alcoholic." Although my search wasn't exhaustive, I came up rather empty-handed. I found several new, modern, non-AA approaches to sobriety during my search. I scanned through their websites and saw words like *rehab*, *detox*, *addiction*, and *recovery* glaring back at me. It didn't feel right. I was pretty sure I didn't need recovery and wasn't an addict. What I *was* was stubborn: the language of addiction and recovery didn't fit me, and I was not willing to pursue a path that didn't fully resonate.

Empty-handed and defeated, I realized I had two choices: call myself an alcoholic and grasp onto the resources provided by both the traditional and modern recovery communities, or keep doing what I was doing. Neither seemed to be a favorable option. Forcing myself into a box just because it was the only box available did not feel empowering or productive.

THE PROBLEM WITH PROBLEM-FOCUSED THINKING

Like it or not, the brand of sobriety has become synonymous with addiction and recovery, making the lifestyle appear both unattainable and unattractive to nonaddicted drinkers. This point of view was further solidified by the formation of Alcoholics Anonymous (AA) in 1935.

From a marketing perspective, the messaging of AA is strong. The organization created clear language and community and—intentionally or not—put its claim on the term "sobriety." While this well-defined association has been invaluable for the many participants of twelve-step programs, it also created an air of exclusivity, making a sober lifestyle appear to be an option only to those with an addiction. For many outside of the organization, sobriety is seen as a necessary treatment for problematic drinkers, not an empowering choice available to anyone and everyone.

For me, AA didn't seem like the right fit for exploring abstinence because entering "the rooms" (as twelve-step meeting places are called in the AA community) and initiating the first step (an admission that you are powerless over alcohol) did not feel in alignment with my personal truth. I was not powerless over alcohol. I *could* quit drinking; I just couldn't see a clear vision of what my life would look like without alcohol in a world that seemed to revolve around booze. For many like me, it is a feeling of incongruity with existing options combined with a fear of the unknown that causes us to hesitate to explore sobriety, not the inability to maintain it.

Although I could have gone for some accountability and encouragement, I didn't physically need help to quit drinking. What I needed was help navigating the world alcohol-free and the courage to create a new life without the confines of alcohol in my way. Because these were not the direct promises of AA or any other recovery program I saw, I quickly became discouraged. If I didn't fit in with the traditionally sober folks or with the drinkers, where did I belong?

All those years ago, my truest desire was to find someone who would say to me what I am saying to you now: **You don't need to have a problem with alcohol for it to be a problem in your life.**

It's true. You can quit drinking void of a problem, a rock bottom, a dire health concern, or a moral reasoning. You can quit drinking without the need for rehab, detox, twelve steps, or a sponsor. You can just quit. For any reason. At any time. You can quit because alcohol is no longer serving you. You can quit because you don't like the way drinking makes you feel or behave. You can quit because, like me, you sense that alcohol is holding you back from being the best, most authentic, successful version of yourself.

If you're like me, you've started to sense that alcohol is creating barriers to living the life you long for. If you feel like alcohol is in any way holding you back from expressing your truest potential in even one single area of your life, alcohol is *absolutely* a problem. I invite you to see this not as an admission of defeat or a burden to bear but as a tremendous point of clarity.

YOU DON'T HAVE A PROBLEM, YOU HAVE AN OPPORTUNITY

If you've found yourself questioning your relationship with alcohol but are afraid to lean into your curiosity because you're fairly certain that you don't have an addiction, I invite you to consider a new truth: What if your curiosity is entirely related to the possibility available for you in a life that is not punctuated with drinking? How would it feel to consider that your intuition is gently nudging you not to recognize a problem, but rather to seize a palpable opportunity?

What if that tiny voice inside that's been urging you to reconsider your relationship with alcohol is, in fact, trying to alert you that you are meant for more than what you can accomplish under the hazy trance of alcohol? Consider this your permission slip to daydream about how free you might feel if you didn't invest time thinking about booze, drinking, or recovering mentally and physically from alcohol. How would that feel?

It's time that we rewrite the limiting social narrative that sobriety is some sort of exclusive club for individuals who cannot control their drinking. This narrow, fear-based way of thinking is not serving you, me, or anyone else, for that matter. This way of thinking is doing nothing but keeping you stuck in your current lifestyle, when you have the opportunity to achieve so much more.

unbottle your potential

Asking Better Questions

All those years ago, I was asking myself if I had a problem with alcohol, and I know now that this was the wrong question. Yet, Do I have a problem? is the most obvious question because it's the question we've been conditioned to ask. I remember seeing a meme that said, "People who don't have a problem with alcohol don't ask if they have a problem with alcohol."

I call bullshit. You see, I was questioning if I had a problem only because it was the popular narrative society had sold to me. Society had spoon-fed me the Do I have a problem? question, and it never occurred to me that I could come up with far better questions to ask when it came to my relationship with alcohol. During the past five-plus years as a nondrinker and now as a coach for women who want to explore elective sobriety, I've found far more productive and helpful questions to ask that have helped me along my journey. Here is an inexhaustive list of some of those better questions. I recommend you set some time aside to journal your answers to each of these questions:

How has alcohol become problematic in my life? Consider how alcohol and your relationship with alcohol have made your life inconvenient, difficult, or uncomfortable. In my own life, alcohol had become problematic because I was spending far too much time consumed with trying to figure it out and beating myself up for "failing." Even though I couldn't necessarily prove it, I could intuit that alcohol was ultimately affecting my mood and ability to show up fully in my work and relationships. Further, I no longer liked who I was as a drinker. I was a superficial, watered-down, judgmental person with a chip on my shoulder. I also had the recurring intuition that, with alcohol in the foreground of my existence, I was not able to express my true potential in any area of my life. Operating from this space didn't feel good. Admitting that I didn't feel good and that alcohol was somehow connected to this mediocre feeling was enough for me to label alcohol as "problematic" in my life, even though I didn't "have a problem."

Is alcohol robbing me of valuable time? Take a minute to roughly add up the hours you spend each week contemplating when you will drink (and how much), planning for alcohol-fueled activities, drinking, and recovering from drinking. When I completed this exercise, it was clear that I was investing massive amounts of time in my relationship with alcohol when I could have been spending some of those hours pursuing my goals.

Is alcohol depleting my physical and mental energy? Although it's difficult to understand precisely how much drinking is affecting your physical and mental capacity until you know what it feels like to be fully functional, create a rough estimate of how often you feel lethargic, unmotivated, foggy, anxious, or irritable after drinking. Add these hours to the number above to get a loose idea of how many valuable hours you are losing to alcohol each week.

Would my life be better without alcohol? This is perhaps the most important question. When I asked myself this question, the answer was nuanced. I knew there would be a knowledge gap where life would feel difficult without alcohol. I'd become so accustomed to the ways alcohol flowed seamlessly into my life that I knew removing it would leave a temporary void. I understood explicitly that there would be a tender period of relearning and confusion. Yet I also knew that surely, as intelligent, savvy, and capable as I was, I could figure out how to get along in life without drinking being in the picture. I sensed that what I found to fill the void would be nothing short of miraculous. And I was right.

Throw aside your fears and imagine for a moment what your life would be like if you had the confidence to navigate the world without alcohol and show up for your life hangover-free. How would you feel each day? How might you show up differently for your relationships and responsibilities?

CHAPTER 2

The Myth of Moderation

Debunking the Lore of Having "Just a Few"

I spent most of 2016 trying to figure out alcohol. Since I had confirmed that I wasn't an alcoholic, I was hell-bent on making moderation work because the thought of complete abstinence scared the shit out of me. Over the course of a year, I tried every trick in the book to figure out moderation:

> ... I took a short break to "reset" my tolerance and desire to drink.

> ... I made a master plan for when to drink and when to abstain.

> ... I set limitations on what I would drink and how many drinks I would have.

> ... I tried drinking on a full stomach and committed to having a glass of water between each cocktail.

In the end, moderation seemed like more work than freedom. More often than not, my innocent attempts to moderate would fail, and I'd go from intending to have *just a few* to indulging in *a few too many*. I'd spend the next day moping on the couch with just enough of a hangover to keep me from doing anything productive.

During my quest for moderation, I tried cleanses and detoxes, resets and challenges. Each effort seemed to garner the same result: while I drank less for a while, I'd eventually return to my previous patterns. Attempting to moderate also resulted in far too many hours obsessing over when I would drink and how much. Then I'd beat myself up for not being more disciplined when my plans went awry. While I was extremely hopeful, attempting to moderate turned out to be a tremendous waste of my mental energy and effort. Ultimately, my attempts at moderation were a continuous and major blow to my self-confidence.

THE FETISHIZATION OF MODERATION

If you're like most social drinkers who have tried to renegotiate their relationship with alcohol, you've probably fantasized about the possibility of training yourself to be a moderate, every-now-and-then, take-it-or-leave-it type of drinker. You've likely looked at other people who moderate their alcohol intake with apparent ease and felt envious, wondering, Why can't I just drink like so-and-so? Like me, you've probably mulled over the many tactics you could employ to *become* a moderate drinker. I'd agree, the idea of flipping some magical switch that allows you to be a casual drinker does sound rather lovely at first, but rest assured, it's a lot more difficult than it sounds and is ultimately a subconscious strategy we use to keep ourselves small.

When we fetishize something, we make it almost godlike. What could be more godlike than believing that one single substance could be responsible for both elevating our happiness and subduing our misery? This is precisely the pedestal we've placed alcohol on. It's no wonder we're hesitant to remove such a seemingly magical substance from our lives. We fear, on a visceral level, that we'll be without the thing that seems to hold our lives together. With the rest of the world shouting about how much we *need* alcohol to relax and cut loose, it's no wonder we hold on to the fantasy that we can keep alcohol in our lives, if only in some little, moderate way.

Now this isn't to say that moderation itself is a myth. Having a moderate relationship with alcohol *is* possible. You surely know plenty of people who moderate. Moderation isn't as easy or glamorous as it sounds, and some of us just aren't built for it innately. I understand that this might not be what you want to hear, but stay with me.

In this chapter, we'll look at the common myths you may have come to believe about moderation. My goal is to enlighten you about the ways we've built moderation up as the ultimate fantasy when it comes to alcohol and offer you an alternative way of thinking.

MYTH 1: ANYONE CAN MODERATE

You can do absolutely anything you put your mind to. However, some activities will require more of your brainpower than others. One of these activities might be moderation.

You no doubt know many people who seem to moderate naturally. It can be easy to compare their behaviors to yours and wonder where you went wrong and subsequently beat yourself up for not having more self-control. When it comes to moderation, the comparison trap can be a defeating thought pattern. Avoid the urge to compare yourself to your acquaintance who seems to always moderate with ease. They are not you, and if there's one thing I've learned, it's that you never know who is secretly dissatisfied with their current relationship with alcohol.

When I was originally trying to wrap my mind around why I, an intelligent, capable woman, was having so much trouble mastering moderation, I came across a helpful concept I want to share with you. The concept is a set of archetypes popularized by author Gretchen Rubin, who posits that we are all naturally moderators or abstainers. If you resonate with other typologies like the Enneagram or Myers-Briggs, Rubin's explanation might appeal to you. *(You can read the full article by visiting the resources webpage for this book: amandakuda.com/unbottledresources.)*

Some of us are not intended to be moderators. If you're one of these people, moderation is not something you can easily train yourself into. But, if you're like me, having a better understanding of these two archetypes might make the decision to abstain seem much more empowering.

Here are some traits of moderators and abstainers, as explained in Rubin's analysis. As you read, keep in mind that identifying your archetype is about what comes most naturally to you, not what you are fetishizing.

MODERATORS

"Do better when they avoid absolutes and strict rules."

"Find that occasional indulgence heightens . . . pleasure and strengthens . . . resolve."

ABSTAINERS

"Find it far easier to give something up *altogether* than to indulge *moderately*."

"Exhaust [themselves] by debating, 'Today, Tomorrow? Does this time "count"? Don't I deserve this?' etc."

"Have trouble stopping something once [they've] started."

"Aren't tempted by things [they've] decided are off-limits."

When I read Rubin's descriptions, it all made sense. I had always been an all-or-nothing type. I'm exercising either consistently on a regular schedule or not at all. Show me a plate of cookies: fine. Invite me to eat from the plate of cookies, and I'll end up having three.

Learning about these abstainers and moderators was tremendously freeing for me because it released me from the shame and blame I'd been placing on myself as someone failing to moderate. If you've been lusting over a moderate relationship with alcohol, consider the possibility that you could find extreme freedom in abstinence because it's what comes more naturally to you.

When I finally made the decision that alcohol was a no for me, it freed up an astonishing amount of mental space and allowed me to use my intellectual bandwidth to contemplate much more pressing matters. While I initially saw abstinence as a burden, I realized that it was actually an incredibly freeing gift.

MYTH 2: MODERATION IS JUST A DECISION YOU MAKE

Early on, I decided that I could will my way to moderation. I thought it was as easy as making the decision and having the self-discipline to stick to it. But in addition to the possibility that you may just be an abstainer rather than a moderator, there are also two other limiting factors at play when it comes to moderating alcohol.

First, willpower is a limited resource. You employ willpower throughout your day when you drag yourself from bed rather than hitting snooze, when you eat a piece of fruit instead of a muffin, when you refrain from road rage on your way to the office, or when you bite your tongue during an aggravating conversation.

The fact of the matter is, by the time it's wine o'clock each afternoon or time for Friday evening happy hour, it would be a miracle if you had any willpower left. With your willpower depleted, it's far more likely that you'll succumb to the temptation of having a drink.

It is normal for your willpower to be depleted by the time you're charged with deciding whether or not to have a drink. If you rely on willpower alone to guide your decision, you're ultimately setting yourself up for a massive mental struggle.

Second, alcohol is not intended to be moderated. You're dealing with a dependency-causing substance here—a substance that is particularly formulated to loosen up your inhibitions. Thus, while you might have the best of intentions to moderate, it's a lot easier to convince yourself it's okay to have another once you're slightly lubricated.

We've made up the story that failing to master moderation makes us a failure. We look to examples of other people who manage to abstain or moderate under what we think are similar conditions, but the reality is we're probably holding ourselves to unrealistic expectations.

MYTH 3: YOU CAN RESET YOUR ALCOHOL TOLERANCE

Ages ago, I had a wishful notion that a short break from booze would be enough to reset my tolerance to alcohol and magically transform me into a moderate drinker. I'm willing to bet you've had similar thoughts or have even given it a try. There is no shortage of quick-fix resets and challenges out there led by well-meaning individuals wanting to nudge you toward a healthier lifestyle.

In my coaching practice, most of the women I work with have tried to use a reset to transition into moderation and found little success. In fact, there's a controversial notion that you cannot reset your consumption threshold. Under this paradigm, taking a break does not reset you to your original drinking capacity but rather to the last marker in the sand. Although you might moderate and feel like a "lightweight" for a while, eventually, most of the women I coach report going back to their former tolerance level and drinking just as much as they did before. Among the women I have coached, this has been true across the board, no matter how long a break they have taken.

Further, as you'll learn as you continue reading this book, abstinence alone isn't enough to significantly change your relationship with alcohol. Therefore, if you've been trying to change your relationship with alcohol using a method rooted primarily in abstinence, you've likely experienced disappointing results.

MYTH 4: EVERYTHING IN MODERATION

You've heard it before: "everything in moderation," right? It's a tricky little saying that we've adopted as gospel to justify our behaviors and habits. Although it's not my mission to create a culture of abstinence, let's look at the facts: Alcohol is ethanol mixed with sugar so that you can tolerate the taste. It is simply not good for you.

As a society, we've glorified alcohol and the moderation of drinking as a way to make right our desire to integrate it into our lives. Why, I wonder, do we so desperately yearn to master the art of consuming sugared-up ethanol at a moderate rate?

I, too, used to be hopeful about someday having a moderate relationship with alcohol. If you're like me, you've also fantasized about the day when you could enjoy a single glass of wine with your friends or sip a cold margarita on a warm day without going overboard. Of course, drinking less is better for you than continuing to drink at a heavy rate. However, when it comes to a toxic substance that is a known dependency-causing carcinogen and depressant, it's confusing to consider why we've made moderating it seem so valuable.

Although there are mixed stances on what constitutes moderation, a growing body of research suggests that the levels of alcohol consumption we once assumed were "safe" are not. According to an Oxford University study, there is, in fact, no safe dose of alcohol consumption.

With growing scientific evidence for the dangers of alcohol, I'm constantly disappointed when I see health and wellness professionals promoting a moderate relationship with alcohol. On any given day, you can log on to your social media platform of choice and find a wellness influencer, health coach, or fitness personality glamorizing drinking or giving their "expert" reassurance that life is about balance and that moderate alcohol consumption is healthy. It's not. (See chapter 4 for more on this.) Although I choose to believe these claims are made from a place of well-meaning ignorance, I encourage you to be discerning when considering advice from individuals who promote balance and moderation when it comes to alcohol.

When you think about it, subscribing to the idea that we'd want to integrate even just a little bit of something toxic into our lives doesn't make a lot of sense. Would you take the advice of someone who told you any other drug—say, methamphetamine or even cigarettes—was okay if you were sure to consume it only in moderation? Of course not. In actuality, alcohol is the only drug you have to explain *not* using.

HOW TO BEAT THE MODERATION MONSTER

To be clear, this is not a book on or against moderation. This is a book about achieving your potential. To do that, I'm going to ask you to take some radical approaches to your own growth that you've perhaps been trying to avoid up to this point.

Again, I'm not telling you that moderation isn't possible, but if you've been placing the fantasy of moderation above your potential, it's time to reorganize your priorities. The approaches I share are intended to help you create a life so magnificent that alcohol becomes insignificant and moderation becomes a dream of the past. If you're open to a new approach, follow these steps to bust through the myths of moderation and start down a new path:

Step 1: Get out of your own way. Lovingly, you are your own worst enemy. If you feel like you've been beating your head against a wall trying to figure out how to make alcohol work for you, it's time to try another angle—one that is focused on what you stand to gain by removing alcohol from your life, not what you stand to lose.

Yes, I want you to change your relationship with alcohol on your own terms and in your own time. And I also know that *your own terms* are often a series of sneaky rules you manufacture to keep yourself stuck. I've been doing this long enough to know all the little ways intelligent, capable, well-meaning individuals self-sabotage on this journey, and it typically begins with trying to make their own rules. This is an invitation to get out of your own way.

Step 2: Ditch the f-word. This is full permission to remove the word *forever* from your current vocabulary. Although we're going to shift the focus away from moderation, I want to be clear that I'm also *not* asking you to commit to giving up alcohol forever. Even if you'd like to get to a place where alcohol is no longer a part of your life, I find that *forever* can be an intimidating commitment. When we're intimidated, we tend to catastrophize and future-trip, creating painful projections of how awful it will be to be sober in Italy or on our honeymoon or on the beach in Mexico.

Getting caught up in a fearful story about what it would look like to never ever drink again is a great way to stir up your inner rebel and convince yourself to toss in the towel altogether. For now, ditch the f-word; we'll talk about a more sustainable, less intimidating commitment in step 4.

Step 3: **Quit the quick fixes.** There is no magic pill for changing the way you drink. Release the notion that you're going to change your drinking via some reset, challenge, or cleanse. Short-term solutions rarely produce long-term results. If you've been lured into the fantasy that a short-term break can change your relationship with alcohol, you're not alone. The results (or lack thereof) have probably left you frustrated and feeling like a failure; you're not.

Quick fixes rarely work because abstaining from alcohol alone isn't enough to change your relationship with it. Most quick fixes rely on counting days, and—to be frank—almost anyone can power their way through a fourteen- or thirty-day challenge. Do yourself a favor and stop falling for well-intentioned, too-good-to-be-true marketing campaigns. Here's what to do instead . . .

Step 4: **Commit and make it nonnegotiable.** I've asked you to avoid the extremes of "forever" and "quick fixes," as these approaches typically backfire. Instead, I recommend that you commit to taking a challenging yet achievable break from alcohol and making that break nonnegotiable. That means no cheat days or reward days.

Here's why: confidence comes from commitments you make and keep. If you create an on-again, off-again relationship with alcohol, your confidence in yourself and your abilities will begin to wane. Therefore, I encourage you to commit—*really* commit—to taking a ninety-day break from booze. I believe in you, and I believe you have something more magnificent to give the world than you can offer as a drinker. You deserve to give yourself a chance.

Ninety days may seem like a long time. Yet, as we'll learn in the upcoming chapters, you didn't get yourself into an uncomfortable relationship with alcohol overnight, so you can't expect to change that relationship overnight either.

There Will Never Be a Convenient Time to Take a Break from Alcohol

There will always be a celebration to toast or a sorrow to drown. There will always be a wedding, a vacation, a happy hour, a sunny day. You will never run short of reasons to drink.

The most convenient time to take a break from alcohol is the day your desire to earnestly pursue your potential outweighs your desire for comfort and complacency.

Step 5: **Do the work.** Your relationship with alcohol is more complex than how much you drink and how often. Drinking alcohol is a behavior, and behaviors are controlled by beliefs. To rewire a behavior, you must simultaneously work on rewiring your beliefs. This will be the focus of the upcoming chapters.

Throughout this book, I'm going to introduce you to many new ways of thinking and behaving that may feel counterintuitive, challenging, or even too easy. I might ask you to question ancient belief systems or explore possibilities that feel uncomfortable. As resistance arises, notice it and fight the urge to skip steps, activities, or concepts. Embark on this journey with an open mind. This is not about punishing or depriving yourself but about opening the space to pursue new opportunities. If you want to start living differently, you must start believing and doing differently. The steps I outline in this book were created through personal trial and error, years of intense study, and the coaching of thousands of sober-curious individuals just like you. I invite you to dive in with an inquiring mind and commit to doing the work.

unbottle your potential

Debunking the Myths of Moderation

Which approaches to moderation have you tried? Realistically, how successful have these approaches been?

How much mental energy have you invested in thinking about, obsessing over, or fetishizing moderation? Be honest: Would that mental energy be better used elsewhere?

After learning about the moderator and abstainer archetypes, which archetype do you most identify with? Have you been trying to fit yourself into an unnatural lifestyle?

How, if at all, have you compared yourself to others or beat yourself up over the concept of moderation? Are you willing to release any self-judgment and consider another approach to changing your relationship with alcohol?

Are you willing to get out of your own way? For the next ninety days, would you be willing to put aside your own limiting beliefs and fears and commit fully to doing the work that could actually help you start living up to your potential by transforming your relationship with alcohol?

Your relationship with alcohol is not unlike any other relationship in your life. It has grown and morphed over time and will require time, attention, and intention to transform. Yet unlike human relationships (healthy ones, at least), your relationship with alcohol is one-sided. Alcohol won't be going to therapy or changing its ways. That means the work is on you.

Moderation is like hooking up with a toxic ex-lover who keeps coming back around attempting to seduce you. The opportunity to try your hand at moderation will feel enticing, perhaps even dangerous and exhilarating. You may find yourself using the tired excuses of "just this once" or "this time will be different." Don't fall for it. Just as a hookup with a toxic ex-lover can shatter your confidence and self-worth, so, too, can a hookup with booze.

In the next chapter, we'll start to reconcile your relationship with alcohol by diving into your love story with alcohol. We'll unpack the ways in which you've romanticized the relationship. Often, once we can see our own delusional fantasy from the outside looking in, it becomes easier to let the fantasy go.

CHAPTER 3

Alcohol: A Love Story

Understanding Your Subconscious Relationship with Alcohol

My love affair with alcohol began innocently enough. I was a naive, self-conscious young woman who wanted nothing more than to fit in with my peers. To be clear: I did *not* naturally fit in and was certainly not considered cool (although I desperately wanted to be). From a young age, I remember having the distinct feeling that I didn't belong—this inexplicable inner knowing that I thought differently than the other kids my age. By the time I reached adolescence, I was a gawky, awkward girl with bad skin, no boobs, and several inches of height on most of the boys in my grade. I grew up in an extremely small town where social status mattered, and my family had none. My parents divorced when I was in elementary school, and my single mother worked her ass off to provide for my brother and me. Because I was painfully aware of my social shortcomings yet full of aspiration, I fought hard to earn a place on the fringe of the cool crowd. I developed a keen sense of humor, worked hard academically, and thrust myself into activities like dance and cheerleading, where I naturally excelled.

The thing is, I never felt like I was good enough. My family didn't live in a nice house or have money to buy the latest clothes. We were on every type of government assistance available, and my mom cleaned my dance teacher's house to pay for my lessons. I spent most of my early adolescence being teased and bullied by mean girls (who I badly wanted to be friends with, by the way) and was never asked on a date or to a dance. Even though I put on a good show, my self-esteem was lower than low. So when I realized that most of my peers were partying on the weekends, I reluctantly decided to play along, hoping it would be my ticket to finally fitting in.

It only took a couple of frozen strawberry daiquiris for me to realize that alcohol was a magical elixir that temporarily subdued my anxieties and insecurities. In my mind, alcohol helped me conquer my fears and confidently mingle with the kids I thought were cool. Before I knew it, I'd gone from a nerdy goody-goody to a Party Girl with no intention of turning back. I was smitten, and so my love affair with alcohol began.

I eagerly carried my newfound Party Girl alter ego with me to college, where—for the first time ever—I felt free to be whoever I wanted to be. I set out to create a new version of reality, and I romanticized my budding relationship with alcohol as my key to success. I spent my twenties dedicated to my social life, glamorizing each drunken night as a massive success.

Even though my relationship with alcohol was considered normal for a coming-of-age woman, it was also utterly and completely toxic. In my fantasy, I believed alcohol helped me become more confident, flirtatious, and outgoing. Weekend after weekend, I gave away my power to alcohol. I was thoroughly convinced that I could not be fun, cool, or popular on my own; in my mind, alcohol was a necessary evil.

As my love affair with alcohol progressed, I learned that alcohol was also a useful emotional anesthetic capable of numbing a variety of impermissible emotions ranging from anxiety to anger to heartbreak. Essentially, alcohol became my cure-all in every area of my life where I felt unable to be vulnerable or cope. Booze became my social lubricant and my emotional crutch.

Of course, my relationship with alcohol wasn't all roses. There were plenty of times when I ended up saying or doing things I regretted. I put myself in a ridiculous number of risky situations and acted more or less recklessly for the better part of a decade. There were nights when alcohol took hold of my emotions, guiding me toward temper tantrums and breakdowns. There were days I spent hopelessly hung over, clinging to a toilet or draped listlessly across my sofa. My inner Party Girl's lesser qualities included arrogance, insensitivity, selfishness, pettiness, and self-importance, just to name a few.

Yet it was all too convenient to write off the consequences of drinking. I can't tell you how many times I uttered the half-hearted phrase "I'm never drinking again," only to forgive alcohol's transgressions just in time for the weekend. I stayed in this toxic loop with alcohol for more than a decade, always chasing the thrill of the highs and conveniently forgetting the depths of the lows.

When the allure of the love affair began to fade, I struggled to cut alcohol out of my life because of how heavily I had romanticized my relationship with it. **For most of us, it is our delusional fantasy about alcohol that makes it so difficult to quit, not our inability to do so.** We've all fallen victim to the fairy-tale narrative that says alcohol has a magical ability to solve all our problems without any consequences. We are a society in a one-sided relationship with a substance that has no intention or ability to actually give us what we desire.

Understanding how you've subconsciously romanticized alcohol is essential to changing your drinking. Why? Most of your actions are fueled by your thoughts . . . and not your conscious thoughts, but your subconscious thoughts. These are the sneaky, somewhat irrational thoughts that play in a loop in the back of your mind. If we fail to bring these thoughts to the forefront, to acknowledge and debunk them, they will continue to dictate our behaviors. In this chapter, we'll get to the bottom of the fantasies that have been driving your relationship with alcohol.

WHAT'S YOUR FANTASY?

We all have elaborate fantasies about how and why we *need* alcohol, along with a romanticization of who alcohol allows us to be. Because we've been crafting this fantasy in our heads for a lifetime, it's often difficult to discern what our fantasies about alcohol are, when these fantasies began . . . and how we've become so inexplicably caught up in them.

The first step to unraveling your complicated, over-romanticized relationship with alcohol is to get clear on the fantasies you've fallen into. If you're like me, you probably hold some pretty commonly romanticized beliefs about alcohol and how it benefits you.

Socially, I believed booze was responsible for making me more outgoing, sexy, sophisticated, and fun. Emotionally, I thought alcohol was useful for when I wanted to feel less anxious, heartbroken, overwhelmed, or frustrated. In my fantasy, alcohol helped me exaggerate the attractive parts of my personality and dilute the parts that were undesirable. Again and again, we turn to alcohol as a magical elixir that can both elevate our joy and drown our sorrow.

And yet these fantasies didn't just pop into my head with my first sip of alcohol. Of course not. No intelligent person would willingly ingest poison without some previous belief that there would be a reward. This is where things get tricky. You see, we rarely account for the fact that our subconscious beliefs about alcohol began long before we began drinking. We've actually been collecting data about the various use cases for alcohol for most of our lifetimes. Much like our idealization of love began long before we started dating (most likely with fairy tales and Disney movies), our romanticization of alcohol began ages before we started drinking, by observing others.

Observing Alcohol

We all knew about alcohol long before we began to drink it. Yet most of us fail to recognize precisely how long we've been making subconscious interpretations about alcohol and how powerful these deep-seated beliefs can be when we're trying to change a behavior.

Depending on the type of household you grew up in, you've probably been observing others interacting with alcohol since your formative years. I think about the silver and blue cans of special sodas my uncles drank around the barbecue grill and the time I innocently took a swig of one of those special sodas only to realize it was lukewarm beer. I remember the strawberry wine coolers my mom sometimes kept in the fridge for a treat after she mowed the lawn or the bottle of vodka my former stepmother smuggled in her purse when she relapsed into addiction. Each of these moments was a mere blip on the map of my childhood. I'd never recount them to you as significant memories, yet each observation took on a subtle meaning that dictated my future perception.

For instance, watching my uncles gather around the grill over a few cold ones gave weight to the idea that drinking creates community. The fact that my uncles liked beer while I found it disgusting subtly cemented drinking as a privilege reserved for adults.

My mom's indulgence in the occasional malt beverage on a warm day verified that alcohol was good for relaxing.

Even my firsthand experience observing my stepmother's relapse into alcoholism created a data point. Later in life, I found myself comparing my drinking to hers as a checkpoint. As long as I wasn't sneaking alcohol or drinking on a daily basis, I figured I was doing okay. She and my father later divorced, but the negative experience of watching a woman I loved and admired sink to her demise was enough to keep me away from the peer pressure to drink until late in my teen years. When I did begin drinking, I made a silent vow that I'd never let myself get *that bad*.

What makes our relationship with alcohol even more nuanced is the shameless glamorization of alcohol in most of the messages we receive. Of course, we've all had health classes where we were taught about the dangers of drinking or observed others suffering the dark consequences of addiction, either in real life or in the media. Yet our understanding of the risks associated with drinking pales in comparison to our desire to experience the glamorous benefits we've been sold.

The Carrie Bradshaw Effect

When I was seventeen, I began religiously devouring the HBO series *Sex and the City*. Each weekend, I'd hunker down with Carrie, Samantha, Charlotte, and Miranda, fantasizing about what it would be like to leave behind my small town for an exciting life in the big city.

Carrie Bradshaw elevated my standards for what it meant to be a *cool girl*. She was sexy, successful, confident, and independent. She had my dream job as a writer and a glamorous big-city life filled with fabulous outfits, fanciful nights out on the town, and handsome men practically lining up to date her.

Any would-be Carrie Bradshaw type could see what brought her character to life: a quirky wardrobe accented with Louboutin heels and a fancy cocktail. I'm pretty sure *Sex and the City* single-handedly made the cosmopolitan martini the "it" drink of the early 2000s. As an impressionable young woman, I did what I could to embody Carrie's persona. While I couldn't afford designer clothing and cosmos, I could afford vodka and strawberry slushies, and just like that, my pursuit of becoming Carrie Bradshaw began.

Messages about alcohol are all around us, sneakily creating imprints about its value in our subconscious minds. I grew up in an incredibly small Midwestern town where there was absolutely nothing highbrow about drinking, but in my coming-of-age, a show like *Sex and the City* made drinking appear sexier, chicer, edgier, and more sophisticated than I'd believed it to be before.

An Ongoing Affair

I carried on the Party Girl charade throughout my twenties, slowly upgrading my social lifestyle along the way. I traded cheap vodka and skunky beers for mediocre wine and proper cocktails. As a young professional still intent on making a Carrie Bradshaw of myself, I slowly started integrating myself into an emerging crowd of young, successful Midwestern socialites.

In this new era of my life, alcohol became a tool for elevated social status. Before I knew it, I'd swapped late nights of clubbing and fraternity parties for an endless string of swanky happy hour spots and posh charity events. Make no mistake, although I upgraded the contents of my glass and the environment in which I was drinking, there was nothing sophisticated about my evolving relationship with alcohol. I continued to imbibe to hide social insecurities and subdue emotional discomfort just as I had in the years before. Like in any other unhealthy relationship, I stuck around because I was too insecure to leave.

Many times during my mid to late twenties, I consciously decided I wanted to drink differently. I made efforts to drink less frequently and in smaller quantities. I upgraded, yet again, to top-label vodka and organic wine in an attempt to be "healthier" about my drinking choices. As my hangovers became less comical and more debilitating, I tried cures and hacks to keep myself in prime condition while still maintaining my Party Girl lifestyle.

The Fleeting Romance

It didn't take me long to realize that rubbing elbows with the see-and-be-seen crowd wasn't all it was cracked up to be. In fact, my pursuit of the elusive Carrie Bradshaw fantasy suddenly felt repetitive, mundane, and shallow. By the time I turned twenty-nine, I was in desperate need of a change. So I followed an interesting chain of serendipitous events and left behind my life in the Midwest for a new, more promising adventure in Austin, Texas.

Although I didn't know much about Austin (I effectively moved there sight unseen), I'd heard it was a cozy, hip town and dreamed of a life where I wouldn't be obligated to a never-ending hamster wheel of hangovers. By this time, I'd all but abandoned my Carrie Bradshaw fantasy and adopted a new life goal of becoming a spiritual yogi type. I was naively certain that the move to Austin was just the thing I needed to foster a seamless transition.

Well, have you ever heard the phrase "wherever you go, there you are"? Suffice to say that although I had a growing spiritual practice, I hadn't quite yet done the work to comfortably transition into this new, more enlightened persona. Little did I know that while Austin does have a thriving wellness scene, more prevalent and familiar was the bustling and boozy social scene of a budding tech town flooded with young professionals with time and money to kill. Like a moth to a flame, I was drawn right back into the Party Girl lifestyle I'd hoped so desperately to be rid of.

For a year and a half I grappled with dueling personalities. One, a Carrie Bradshaw type living the fabulous, carefree life of a Party Girl. The other, a powerful, independent young woman on the verge of a massive spiritual awakening. I tried, albeit unsuccessfully, for months on end to live a double life. During the week, I was an enlightened woman, persistently reading spiritual texts and sharing inspirational quotes in a fleeting attempt to convince myself and the rest of the world that I was serious about my spiritual practice. On the weekends, I reverted to my Party Girl ways, under the delusion that I could achieve balance and have the best of both worlds. Although I wanted more for my life, I simultaneously felt a sense of duty to uphold the Party Girl persona I'd invested more than a decade in bringing to life. There were parts of her that I genuinely thought I liked; I was afraid of who I would be if I let them go. My deepest fear was that I'd be a social outcast. As a young, social single woman, this thought scared the hell out of me.

Realistically, I was in the middle of a major existential crisis, and alcohol was the anesthetic I used to numb the discomfort of teetering on the fragile edge of a transition from my old identity as a Party Girl to embracing my authentic self. I'll cover this more in the second half of this book, but suffice to say I am not the only one who has experienced this phenomenon.

Breakups and Breakthroughs

New Year's Day 2017 was the last time I drank alcohol. I distinctly remember placing my half-empty beer on a table in the crowded bar and walking out with the goal of abstaining from alcohol for just thirty days. Let me be clear: I had no idea this would be my last drink. Making sobriety an ongoing lifestyle was never my intention. Because I wasn't a problem drinker, total abstinence didn't register as an option for me. In the beginning, I thought I'd take a long enough break from drinking to rewire my tendencies. In my fantasy, I'd retrain myself to be a moderate drinker. But what was initially a short break made room for breakthroughs, which led to a full-fledged, completely unintentional, life-changing breakup.

Now it's time for you to unpack your love affair with alcohol and all the subconscious, fantastical ideas that have kept you stuck in this toxic relationship. In working with clients, I find three main benefits to understanding the psychological relationship with alcohol.

First, once you realize and fully embrace that your psychological relationship with alcohol predates your physical relationship, it can make more sense that changing the relationship isn't as easy as abstaining from alcohol.

Second, digging into the fantasies and projections you've created about alcohol—namely, that it's a necessary and deserved evil—will help you understand the depths to which booze has infiltrated your life. It's much easier to release self-judgment when you recognize that it's not only the behavior of drinking that has kept you stuck, but also your subconscious beliefs and mindset *about* drinking that have you running in place.

Third, understanding how you've glamorized alcohol will help you call yourself out on your own crap. I work with incredibly intelligent and capable women in my coaching practice. This often means they're extremely skilled at camouflaging their suboptimal coping patterns. But once they're alerted to their own sneaky forms of self-sabotage, they're more likely to put intention into changing.

TALKING ABOUT YOUR BREAKUP WITH BOOZE

One of the biggest concerns my students have about changing their relationship with alcohol is how they'll tell others they're not drinking. There's a certain anxiety that comes with confessing that you're no longer going to participate in an activity that most other people consider entirely normal. You might worry about what you'll say or how people will take it. Don't worry, I've got you. Here are the steps to confidently and effectively talk about your breakup with booze:

Step 1: **Know your why.** List some of the reasons that you've decided it's time to break up with booze. Choose the top three inarguable reasons (meaning reasons others can't easily push back on because they are personal and true). Avoid using situational whys such as "I'm waking up early" or "I'm driving." Although these things might be true, it's easy to argue for you to *just have one.* If you use an inarguable excuse such as "I don't like the way it makes me feel," others will have a much more difficult time trying to persuade you.

Step 2: **Make a basic script.** Your script should be super simple: "I'm actually not drinking right now because [insert inarguable reason from step 1]." You might also want to add your time frame to this script for clarity. So instead of saying "right now," say "for the next ninety days," "through the end of the year," or "for the summer."

Step 3: **Ask for support.** Believe it or not, people who care about you want to support you, so ask for it. I encourage my clients to be honest and vulnerable when asking for support. See if something like this works for you: "I'm very dedicated to not drinking, but I'm also super nervous and I'd appreciate you supporting me."

Step 4: **Communicate your breakup to an advocate.** Although you'll be pleasantly surprised by how little people notice or even care that you're not drinking, I always encourage my clients to communicate their breakup with booze to an advocate *before* a social outing or event. This might look like sending off a quick text with your version of the following script:

"Hey, I wanted to let you know that I'm taking a ninety-day break from alcohol, and I'm excited about it but also nervous about [name of upcoming social event], and I'd like your support. Can I count on you?"

It's as simple as that. Proactively communicating your goals and needs to someone who cares about you will help you feel more prepared for social situations and keep you from awkwardly fumbling over your words in the moment. Further, preparing a short, simple script will ensure you're ready if and when you feel like sharing with anyone else.

Pro tip: One of the traits I see in newly alcohol-free individuals is a tendency to overshare and offer information that wasn't asked for. For example, if someone asks, "Can I get you something to drink?" they're *not* asking for your current drinking status; they're asking for your drink order. All you need to do is tell them what you do or don't want to drink, not share your current relationship status with alcohol. Think about it like this: if you walked into a restaurant alone after a breakup and the host or hostess asked if you'd be dining alone, you wouldn't share all the details of your recent romantic woes, would you? Probably not. Why make it any different with alcohol?

What not to say: At some point in your alcohol-free journey, you'll reach a point of euphoria where you'll want to shout the wonders of sobriety from the rooftop. You'll feel the urge to let everyone in on the dirty little secrets you know about alcohol and share how wonderful life has been since you broke up with booze. Not so fast, friend. Talking about alcohol can be a delicate, if not disarming, conversation for people who aren't quite yet willing to reconsider their relationship with drinking. It's important that you tread lightly. The way you share about sobriety can create either intrigue or contempt toward the topic. As the old saying goes, actions speak louder than words. Focus your attention on demonstrating the joys of living alcohol-free versus sharing them (unless directly asked).

LUSTING OVER BOOZE

A few months into our work together, my client Suzy shared that she'd started daydreaming about alcohol. Slowly, she began to minimize all the negative aspects of her relationship with alcohol and fantasize about all the ways drinking made her feel good. She confessed that she imagined how nice it would feel to slip away from the reality of her emotions for just a few minutes in the evening. She wondered if perhaps she was being too strict with herself and maybe could try having just one at the end of the day.

I recognized Suzy's pattern immediately: she was lusting over booze and trying to legitimize a fling. It's a common thing to do after any breakup, and it's precisely why many people end up back in crummy romantic relationships that didn't serve them in the first place.

In my work as a coach, I've seen that the act of lusting over booze is a clear sign you're not quite ready to try your hand at the relationship again. Lusting indicates you're trying to feed an urge; this rarely ends well.

My goal is to help my clients reach a neutral relationship with alcohol. At that point, most people no longer have an interest in a relationship at all. In my opinion, this is an incredibly powerful and empowering place to be. This is what I want for you, too. I want you to heal your relationship with alcohol so that it's no longer a romanticized love story that never quite delivers. I want to help you fall more in love with yourself and your life so that having a fling with alcohol is no longer appealing.

unbottle your potential

Getting to the Root of Your Romanticized Relationship with Alcohol

What is your "love story" with alcohol? Sit down and take as much time as you need to journal out your story in narrative form. Document where you were mentally and physically at each point in your relationship with alcohol so that you can better understand the various ways you used it as a cure-all. For inspiration, you can look back at how I outlined my story throughout this chapter. I recommend you break your story up into significant life cycles (your teen/college years, young professional years, and so on).

Most of my clients report that this process is extremely cathartic and eye-opening. Looking at your story through the lens of your relationship with alcohol will inevitably point to some common themes and areas of opportunity for growth.

What are your fantasies about alcohol? Explore the beliefs you have about alcohol that have given it power in your life. How have you used alcohol to help you exaggerate perceived positive characteristics in social situations? Similarly, how have you turned to alcohol to help you avoid perceived negative emotional states? If you get stuck, try completing some of the following prompts:

- **I believe alcohol helps me become more . . .** (While completing this prompt, consider specifically how you've used alcohol as a social lubricant.)

- **I feel alcohol helps me to be less . . .** (While completing this prompt, consider specifically how you've used alcohol as an emotional crutch.)

- **Without alcohol, I'm afraid I won't be able to . . .**

How did you observe alcohol during your formative years? Think back to your childhood and adolescence. How did you observe alcohol consumption in your immediate family unit? How did you observe alcohol in your extended family unit? Can you think of how these observations helped you build a subconscious case for romanticizing alcohol in adulthood?

Many of my clients begin this exercise struggling for memories. If this is the case, don't force this part of the exercise. Opening your awareness to these memories is often enough to call them forward in their own time. Don't be surprised if you recall an early observation of alcohol days later while you're in the shower or out for a walk. If this happens, return to your journal and jot it down.

Like me, you may have observed the ugly side of drinking through a family member who grappled with addiction or went to dark or violent places while drinking. If this is your first time processing these memories, please consider working with a therapist or counselor who is prepared to hold space for you.

How have you glamorized alcohol? Consider the role media has played in your glamorized view of drinking. Can you think of characters, influencers, celebrities, or real-life role models who have contributed to your way of thinking about alcohol as a necessary and normal lifestyle habit?

To dive deeper into releasing your story, visit amandakuda.com /unbottledresources to complete my Past Selves Meditation.

As you review your love story with alcohol, please do your best to resist the urge to judge yourself over your past. Release the notion that you *should* have known better. Romanticization is all about living in the projected fantasy versus reality. When we have romanticized a relationship—be it with a substance or a person—it can be difficult to see the suffering we are causing ourselves in real time. And even when we do, it's just as easy to convince ourselves that the perceived positive outcome is worth the suffering. You are a human being having a human experience, and most human experiences come with the opportunity to learn and do better. Picking up this book is a clear indication that you're on the right path.

If you do find yourself stuck in self-judgment or shame about your past, remember this: your past was supposed to happen to you because it did. I believe the memories that make you cringe most happened *for* you and not *to* you. In the end, it was the culmination of these cringeworthy events that created a catalyst for change. You would not be here today reconsidering your toxic relationship with alcohol and committing to achieving your potential if your relationship with alcohol had been pure bliss. Sometimes we need to make ourselves just uncomfortable enough to become open to embracing change. I count it a blessing that your past has led you to this path because this is the path to a new way of being. This is the beginning of a new love story where you start by loving yourself first.

In the next chapter, I'll help you get real about how your romanticized relationship keeps you stuck in a dulled-down version of your life. We'll look at how alcohol's influence has gone beyond the bounds of happy hours and hangovers and begun to limit your potential in all areas of your life.

CHAPTER 4

A Life Dulled by Booze

Acknowledging How Alcohol Is Keeping You Stuck

By the time I reached thirty, I couldn't shake the feeling that it was time to break up with booze. I knew in my gut that drinking was keeping me stuck, but I was having a difficult time articulating precisely how I knew this. Remember, from the outside, it looked like I had it all together. I had a master's degree, a great job, a beautiful home, and a nice car. I also had a vibrant social and dating life, I was fit, I was healthy, et cetera, et cetera, et cetera. At one point, I'd even been named one of the top twenty young professionals under thirty by a posh Midwestern society magazine. It certainly looked like I was thriving.

I'd also doubled down on taking care of myself. I enrolled in therapy, purchased gym and hot yoga memberships, and focused on eating well. I started seeing healers and bodyworkers and even sat with a local shaman to help get myself into physical and spiritual alignment. Spiritually, I grew curious about what was *out there* and started seeking answers outside my physical sight. I traded late-night reality TV binges for self-help books and spiritual texts with the most earnest intention of making my inner world match my new vision for success.

Yet with all the wonderful things happening in my life and the massive amounts of inner and outer work I was doing, I wasn't fulfilled. It's not that I was depressed; I just wasn't happy. I felt stuck, and—what's worse—I felt guilty for feeling stuck. I kept telling myself I *should* just be happy because I lived a privileged life compared to so many others. No matter how many times I tried to talk myself into being grateful for everything I had (which, don't get me wrong, I was), I couldn't shake the feeling that I wasn't quite achieving what I was capable of.

Frankly, I was tremendously frustrated that I felt so off track. After all, I'd invested thousands of hours (and dollars) in my education only to be unsure if my career was even a fit for me. I was doing all the health, wellness, and spiritual things that were supposed to lead to a miraculous and abundant life. Yet I was broke (and in debt up to my eyeballs), single (and brokenhearted after a whirlwind romance), and nearly exhausted from implementing the new positive behaviors I'd added to my life.

Then it hit me: maybe it wasn't about how much I could *add* to my life but what I could *subtract*. I had officially reached capacity, and it was time to start purging. Reluctantly, I looked again at the only real vice I had: drinking. You already know I wasn't keen on the idea of going sober. I was completely blocked by the fact that I wasn't an alcoholic and there didn't seem to be options for me. I was also blindly attached to the romanticized relationship I'd built with booze.

I can't tell you how many times I tried to talk myself out of sobriety as a probable solution. I was headstrong and hell-bent on figuring out a way to make my relationship with alcohol work. Time after time, I ran the math to see if I could find a balance between my life and alcohol, and time after time, the answer was the same: if I sincerely wanted to live my best life, booze had to go.

Atomic Habits author James Clear said it best: "The ultimate form of optimization is elimination. Nothing is more effective than removing the ineffective." No matter how much I tried to fight it, the most ineffective aspect of my life was my relationship with alcohol. Despite my biggest fears about pursuing a life of sobriety, I sensed intuitively that removing alcohol from my life was going to be the catalyst for something miraculous . . . and I was right.

In the last chapter, we took a closer look at the ways in which you romanticize alcohol and make it important in your life. Now it's time to get clear about how, precisely, alcohol has been dulling your life, diluting your potential, and ultimately keeping you stuck.

ALCOHOL STEALS TIME AND ENERGY

On the most basic level, it's easy enough to understand how your relationship with alcohol has robbed you of the time and energy you need to be your best self. If you were to do a quick calculation of how many hours, on average, you spend preparing for boozy events, drinking, and recovering from drinking alone, you'd likely have a humbling idea of just how much of your life you've devoted to alcohol.

Reviewing your history is not an invitation to beat yourself up. I do not believe in the concept of lost time. Rather, I believe every opportunity to change paths comes to us in divine timing. You were led to explore this lifestyle at this exact moment because the time is right for you. Once you have stepped onto the *right* path (the path of your potential), time will expand in your favor, and any perceived lost time will become entirely insignificant.

Competing Internal Voices

From a metaphysical perspective, our internal narrative is guided by two opposing voices, that of the **Inner Critic** (often called the *ego*) and that of our **Inner Guide** (often called *intuition* or the *higher self*).

The Inner Critic represents the voice of criticism, judgment, negativity, lack, and impossibility. The Inner Guide is the voice of encouragement, possibility, abundance, and inspiration.

The Inner Critic thrives on your smallness and stagnation. The Inner Guide thrives on the fulfillment of your potential.

Your Inner Critic often searches for fulfillment from external validation and superficial achievements, while the Inner Guide is fulfilled by internal progress.

When it comes to alcohol, your Inner Critic will always encourage you to drink because it fuels your insecurities and stunts your growth. Drinking also amplifies the voice of the Inner Critic while simultaneously muffling the voice of your Inner Guide.

ALCOHOL CLOUDS CLARITY

In order to become your fullest expression of human potential, you must first have the space to discern what that version of you looks like. Drinking alcohol dilutes clarity, not only in the moment but also longer term. When you drink on a frequent basis, you muffle the connection to your Inner Guide, which is your source of clarity and creativity. Without this connection, you end up following dreams and desires that are not actually your own.

If you've felt the subtle sense that you are on the wrong path but can't quite figure out what the right path looks like, you need clarity, and the fastest way to get it is to create a clear channel of communication with your Inner Guide. Once my private coaching clients finally get alcohol out of the picture, they always marvel at how unclearly they had seen things as drinkers. Their common sentiment is something like this: "I didn't know how much I couldn't see, but now that I see it, I can't unsee it."

ALCOHOL FUELS SELF-DOUBT

Alcohol does a doozy on your inner compass. While drinking muffles the voice of your Inner Guide, it simultaneously amplifies the voice of your Inner Critic. Your Inner Critic is the voice of skepticism, judgment, lack, and fear. When you drink, you give this voice a microphone to amplify its potency. You've surely felt this self-doubt and negativity during an active hangover (some call it *hangxiety*), but you've failed to recognize that regular drinking also increases the power of your Inner Critic over time.

When the voice of the Inner Critic is strong, you are less likely to dream big and take inspired action. Your Inner Critic is constantly deterring you from aiming for your potential in sneaky and subtle ways. If you've ever talked yourself out of pursuing a desire (no matter how logical the reasoning), it is a sure sign your Inner Critic is at work.

ALCOHOL REDUCES MOTIVATION

Even if you identify as a go-getter, achieving your truest potential will still require an entirely new level of motivation. Of course, you've experienced the lackluster feeling you get the day after drinking, when a hangover is in full effect. However, it's unlikely that you are aware of the subtle fog that resides for days after you drink. This residual effect can cause you to move more slowly, think slightly more negatively, and lack the motivation to get things done at your full capacity. Because you are a go-getter, this can be difficult to spot, as you are most likely moving and thinking faster than those around you. Yet it's probable that you're operating at only a fraction of the capacity that you're capable of. Imagine what you could do if you were always operating at maximum motivation, efficiency, and inspiration. You'd be unstoppable.

ALCOHOL ALTERS YOUR BRAIN AND BODY

I was always under the impression that the physical effects of alcohol dissipated around the time my hangover wore off. This was an incredibly naive assumption. Alcohol is ethanol. Ethanol is a toxin. Toxins wreak havoc on the body in ways that are beyond our physical sight and immediate recognition.

In case you missed the memo from junior high health class: Alcohol screws you up on the cellular level. It is a depressant that impairs the functions of all your vital organs. Over time, alcohol degrades your cognitive capacity, interferes with digestion, suppresses your immune system, decreases your sex drive, and increases the intensity of anxiety and depression. These negative consequences aren't just for those who drink heavily. Nope, in fact, multiple health organizations (such as the World Health Organization and the U.S. Department of Agriculture) are tightening up on their prior recommendations when it comes to consuming alcohol.

In an August 2022 episode of his eponymous podcast titled "What Alcohol Does to Your Body, Brain and Health," neuroscientist and Stanford professor Andrew Huberman reviews the findings of several reputable academic studies about the effects of alcohol. They all corroborate the same, unavoidable truth: Although ethanol is a form of alcohol that is technically fit for human consumption, it is still toxic. Alcohol substantially stresses and damages cells, and it is indiscriminate as to which cells it damages and kills.

In other words, even if you drink in moderation—an amount that no one can seem to agree upon—you are still putting your body at risk because you are ingesting poison that disrupts your neural circuits and all the vital organs in your body. Even if you drink in small amounts, the enzyme that breaks down alcohol is forced to work at its maximum capacity.

Yet because most of the negative consequences of drinking increase chronically over time, it's easy to let them go unnoticed. These are not glaring, bold consequences that we see immediately after drinking. It's easy enough to chalk most chronic symptoms of alcohol use up to age or other preexisting health factors. Over time, we become so used to feeling blah that we may not even realize we're not operating at optimum capacity.

It's also important to note that the negative consequences of alcohol don't just disappear once you're no longer buzzed, drunk, or hung over. Because alcohol is a toxin, it interferes with the overall optimal functions of your body for a disturbing amount of time. I like to explain it like this: Think of your body as a funnel. The top of the funnel is where alcohol goes in and creates damage. The bottom of the funnel is where your body repairs itself from the disturbance alcohol created. Most of us—even if only consuming moderately and on occasion—are refilling the top of the funnel (creating more work for the body) before the funnel can empty (repair itself from previous damage)

Alcohol creates chemical and mineral deficiencies in the body that can take many months, if not longer, for the body to recalibrate after alcohol is no longer being consumed. The unfortunate reality I see in many people trying to change their relationship with alcohol is that they don't give themselves a long enough period of abstinence to see any true results. In other words, if you drink consistently, even in moderation, you are never allowing your body to fully repair. Therefore, you will experience subtle negative residual effects that keep you from performing at your best and experiencing the positive benefits of sobriety. So, each time you think, Just one won't hurt, remember that you are refilling the funnel and thus prolonging your wait to achieve homeostasis.

The positive physical effects of removing alcohol range from the subtle—including better sleep, clearer skin, and more energy—to the more profound healing of big-picture health concerns. I loved the physical energy and resiliency I gained from sobriety. After I gave up drinking, fitness became a fast replacement for partying because I suddenly had more energy and motivation to test myself physically. Further, my body recovered much more quickly, allowing me to spend more time in the gym exploring my new livelihood.

Keep in mind that each body processes alcohol differently. The length of time it will take you to fully realize the physical benefits of sobriety will rely greatly on your unique body composition, how often and how much you drank, your lifestyle, and any underlying health conditions. If you don't see some physical improvement after ninety days to six months, you might consider working with a health professional who specializes in helping those living an alcohol-free lifestyle.

Underlying Health Conditions

Although it's difficult to predict just how much drinking alcohol can exacerbate existing health conditions, it certainly doesn't help the cause. For those dealing with chronic issues such as autoimmune conditions, alcohol can sometimes seem like an escape from a world void of solutions. Yet because alcohol negatively impacts the body's overall ability to function and requires a tremendous amount of energy to process, it is important to consider the high probability that drinking is robbing your body of the strength it needs to address other conditions. Therefore, if you've been frustrated with your body's ability to heal and haven't yet committed to removing alcohol from your routine, I'd say it's certainly worth a try.

Debunking "Healthy Drinking"

You're probably hoping this is where I'll reveal the surprising health benefits of a nightly glass of vino. Or perhaps you're wondering if I'll remind you that Jesus Christ himself turned water into wine, which means there must be some tiny benefit to drinking alcohol, right? Wrong. Those antioxidants in wine you read about? A quick Google search will reveal that you can enjoy the same quantity of antioxidants in many fruits without simultaneously ingesting lighter fluid. You may also wonder about organic wine, sugar-free seltzers, or "good for you" cocktails that have trendy supplements like collagen or ashwagandha added.

Here's the deal: Alcohol is alcohol is alcohol. It is a substance with zero nutritional value. The health benefits you've read about are hopeful, at best. The additives and healthy production processes touted by some brands are unsophisticated marketing tactics. In reality, your body spends so much energy processing alcohol, you're unlikely to receive many benefits from any perceived "healthy" alcoholic beverage. You would be much better served investing in health protocols that do not also entail drinking poison. There is absolutely no benefit to drinking alcohol, no way to make alcohol "healthy," and no safe amount of alcohol to consume, full stop.

Body Image and Emotional Eating

While going alcohol-free can help create space for a healthier body, sobriety isn't a quick fix for weight loss. Removing alcohol from your lifestyle is a long game in personal development and healing. This healing may include working through underlying body image issues or emotional and disordered eating. If you find yourself consumed with body image as you embark on this journey, consider seeking the support of a professional.

ALCOHOL LOWERS YOUR ENERGETIC VIBRATION

I was introduced to the concept of energetics when I started getting serious about my spiritual practice. From a metaphysical perspective, everything has energy. This energy is omnipresent yet invisible to the naked eye. For this reason, the study of energetic vibration and frequency is considered rather esoteric, although it is widely accepted in alternative medicine and spiritual traditions.

For example, the Eastern wellness practices of Reiki and acupuncture focus on attuning the body's energetic frequency. Other energetic concepts include the study of the body's aura and chakra system. From a spiritual perspective, meditation and breathwork practices, such as Kundalini, focus on cultivating positive energy in the body. You may have even been introduced to the practice of using crystals or sage or palo santo to clear the energy of a place or person.

The growing popularity of mystical studies on social media has given rise to the use of such expressions as "high vibe" and "low vibe" to describe the energetic frequency of specific people, practices, environments, or experiences. You may have experienced people or environments that cause you to feel energetically drained or stimulated for no specific reason.

You are a vibrational being in a vibrational universe. Everything you see has an energetic vibrational quality, but you've become so good at interpreting vibrations that you hardly realize you're doing it. Most people are utterly unaware that they are, in fact, vibrational beings, highly sensitive to the vibrational experiences around them.

Your own energetic vibration is dictated by your thoughts, actions, feelings, and interactions. In this sense, you have so much more control over your energetic vibration than you realize. Yet we live in a society that encourages us to cheat our way to the feelings we desire. We're taught to fill our voids rather than do the inner work required to achieve our desired emotional states. The most socially acceptable void filler is alcohol.

Alcohol is a depressant. Drinking literally depletes your physical energy, slows you down cognitively, and takes you out of energetic alignment. Of course, we can still function with a lowered energetic vibration, but this is not the optimal state. Unfortunately, most of us have become so accustomed to vibrating at a lower energetic frequency that we are unaware of it.

Vibrate Higher

Every choice you make is an energetic investment. Just like financial investments, energetic investments have either positive or negative returns. Like attracts like. Therefore, if you purposely choose positive energetic investments, you will be rewarded with positive energetic returns, which will increase your personal energetic vibration. Similarly, negative energetic investments will have matching returns. Although alcohol may initially appear to be a positive investment in some instances, remember that alcohol is a depressant; thus, the *overall* energetic return will always be negative.

When you are in energetic alignment, every aspect of your life will improve. You will feel better and become more confident and resourceful. Others who admire your energy will naturally be attracted to your new vibrational state. If you allow yourself to feel good, you will organically attract more people and opportunities that contribute to this good-feeling energy. Further, most people I know who begin to see the benefits of positive energetic investments only desire to make further positive energetic investments in themselves and others. Your choice to vibrate higher will have a ripple effect, not only in your life but in the lives of those around you.

ALCOHOL STUNTS EMOTIONAL GROWTH

Most people use alcohol as an emotional crutch in areas of their lives where they don't feel fully competent to cope. Even if you consider yourself a social drinker, you are most likely still using alcohol to subdue feelings of emotional discomfort, such as anxiety, self-doubt, or overstimulation. In this sense, we use alcohol to cheat our way through situations where we lack emotional skills. When we drink to bypass our emotional experience, we get the illusion that we are mastering a skill when we're just cheating.

Think about it; if you were actually becoming more confident through drinking, eventually you wouldn't need drinking to exude confidence at all. Likewise, if alcohol were actually helping you become less stressed, your stressors would be fully under control the day after you imbibe. In my experience, it's much more likely that you spend the day after drinking wallowing in self-judgment and fighting to subdue amplified anxiety.

Drinking is like a life jacket for your emotions; it keeps you floating on the surface of your emotional experiences under the illusion that you know how to swim. But when you float on the surface, you miss the exhilarating opportunity to experience the true depths of life. Yes, this may keep you from having to grapple with negative emotions, but rest assured, it also blocks you from fully experiencing positive emotions.

Further, when we numb ourselves through negative emotions rather than experiencing them, they become stagnant in the body. Unresolved and unfelt emotions stored in the body can turn into depression and disease. Drinking as a coping mechanism also reinforces a negative, subconscious story that you are not capable of handling these emotions on your own.

Failing to process negative emotions keeps us stuck in negativity. You are deserving of happiness and true relief. The fastest way to get there is to consciously commit to removing any barriers you have to happiness. If you are harboring ages of repressed trauma, anger, sadness, worry, or anxiety, you are assuredly blocking your route to happiness.

Sobriety is an opportunity to show up fully for the emotional life experiences available to you and embrace your competence to do so. This will require some bravery, tenacity, and humility on your part. Remember that you have been cheating at the emotional game for at least as long as you have been drinking. When you begin to operate without the false support of alcohol, there will certainly be uncomfortable and uncertain moments. Bearing through these moments can be some of your biggest teachers and experiences of triumph. I aim to prepare you for these challenges in the coming chapters.

The world is your practice field. Each time you are faced with a social or emotional experience where you might have drunk before, you are reprogramming your mind by choosing to show up. Each time you show up, you take a stand for your self-worth by sending the message that you are indeed capable of withstanding all life's circumstances.

Trust that you would not have been given the ability to experience emotions from sadness and heartbreak to bliss and joy if you were not meant to. You are more emotionally resilient and capable than you give yourself credit for. You have an unlimited capacity to feel your way through all emotional experiences that come your way, even those that seem insurmountable. In fact, you are not only capable but undeniably worthy of experiencing the full spectrum of human emotions available to you. From the depths of extreme sorrow and grief to the highs of unfettered joy and happiness, these emotional experiences are your birthright.

The fullness at which you can experience life is directly related to the level at which you are willing to experience your emotions. Numbing of any kind pulls us out of the emotional experience, disabling us from living life in its fullest form.

ALCOHOL ERODES AUTHENTICITY

As drinkers, we're all presenting dulled-down versions of ourselves. In his book *Alcohol Explained,* my friend William Porter has a brilliant line: "The fact is that whoever you are as a drinker, it is not the real you. It is a poor quality you." As I look back on who I was as a drinker, this blunt analysis could not be truer. Although I *thought* that alcohol brought out a more engaging, carefree version of me, all it did was dilute my brilliance. I was not being my authentic self as a drinker. Hell, I'd put so much effort into becoming a cooler, more socially acceptable version of myself that I hardly knew who my authentic self was, and this started to spill over into my daily interactions. The self I presented was a cheap facsimile of me. It was a hologram of who I thought the world wanted me to be in order to be seen as fun and popular.

You are doing yourself and the rest of the world a tremendous disservice each time you choose to show up as the dull, diluted version of yourself. You are hiding the most unique, honest, and quirky parts of yourself that make you human and incredibly endearing. You are robbing the people around you of experiencing your humanness. True connection is built around humanity. It may feel like alcohol is bringing you closer to people, but it's actually keeping you at a distance from them.

Signs You May Be Out of Authentic Alignment

In most cases, alcohol isn't what pulls us out of authentic alignment. We tend to lose touch with our authentic selves through a series of tiny abandonments made throughout childhood and adolescence as a method of self-preservation. We typically make these micro-abandonments out of fear of perceived punishment or a promise of reward.

For example, maybe someone made you feel ashamed or self-conscious about an interest or hobby, so you stopped pursuing that interest to avoid further shame and embarrassment. Or maybe you were made to feel selfish or frivolous for pursuing an interest that was not considered productive in your family. At a young age, you also may have been rewarded for acting maturely or been required to care for others. You might also resonate with feeling different from those around you and adjusting your personality to better fit in. Many life experiences might cause us to subtly alter our own character in order to be accepted. Yet when we do so, we ultimately set ourselves up for discontent later in life.

Here are some common signs that you might be out of authentic alignment:

- You often find yourself doing or saying what you think will most please others.

- You hide behind armor and avoid vulnerability.

- You don't have hobbies or interests outside of work, family, and your social life.

- You lack creative outlets.

- You choose hobbies or pastimes based on what is cool or most acceptable in your social group versus spending time on activities you enjoy.

- You chose a career based on practicality or esteem versus desire.

- You excel in your career (and most things you do), but you're not fulfilled by the work.

- You feel stuck on a path you're not meant to be on.

- You identify as a people pleaser or perfectionist.

- You've always considered yourself a little weird or different from those around you, and you've put effort into downplaying your more eccentric side to appear *normal*.

- There are things you want to accomplish that you feel guilty or childish for pursuing.

- You downplay your abilities and desires out of the fear of being criticized for being "too much" if you shine as brightly as you are capable of.

Once out of alignment, it's common to turn to the most socially acceptable tool we can find to minimize our feelings of inauthenticity: alcohol. Although drinking may temporarily lessen the discomfort of living inauthentically, the unfortunate reality is that drinking also keeps us from returning to authentic alignment. Alcohol keeps us stuck by muffling our communication with our internal guidance system and limiting our motivation to take action toward fulfilling our dreams. As drinkers, we have trouble returning to our most authentic selves because we're too filled with self-doubt, too short on time, or—frankly—too hung over. Therefore, even if you've heard the nudge of your Inner Guide to start living differently, it's likely you've lacked the courage, confidence, and ambition to do much about it.

If you feel out of alignment with your authentic self and are unable to tap into your dreams and desires, the greatest gift you can give yourself is the gift of clarity. This is the promise of sobriety. Clarity, combined with increased time, energy, and self-confidence, will go a long way in helping you live as your most authentic self, thus achieving your personal potential.

ALCOHOL KEEPS YOU STUCK IN "GOOD ENOUGH"

Alcohol has caused you to settle for mediocre, *good-enough* life circumstances when you are capable of so much more. Each day, you have a choice to take a stand for your potential or take a stand for your complacency. No matter why, how often, or how much you drink, you are beginning to understand that drinking is ultimately a subconscious acceptance of a life dulled by booze.

You are worthy of more than *good enough*. Do not for one more moment let yourself be seduced by the idea that you *should* be happy with what you have. Yes, you can be *grateful* for what you have, but if your current life status is not a reflection of your truest potential, please do not force yourself into complacency.

unbottle your potential

Getting Unstuck

How much time and energy would you gain from sobriety? Do a rough calculation of how many hours—on average— you spend preparing for boozy events, drinking, and recovering from drinking each week. If you've been sober curious for long, take your best guess at accounting for how many mental hours you've lost trying to figure out moderation by thinking about when you'll drink, how much, and how you'll contain yourself when out drinking. Multiply that number by fifty-two for a good idea of how much time you'll have to devote to claiming your potential once alcohol is out of the way.

What are the messages you hear from your Inner Guide? Tap into the loving voice of your Inner Guide. Remember, this is the inner voice of possibility, hope, creativity, abundance, love, and encouragement. It is the voice that has guided you to this book and to your growing curiosity about living alcohol-free. What has that voice suggested is possible for you? Are you willing to believe there might be deep wisdom in this voice?

What are the messages you hear from your Inner Critic? Recall the nagging voice of your Inner Critic; you are likely well acquainted. This is the voice of negativity, doubt, fear, and criticism. It is the voice that frequently causes you to question your desire to grow, change, or improve in any way. It is the voice that suggests you *should* just be happy. It is the voice that asks, Who are you to dream this big dream? It is the voice that discourages you from changing your relationship with alcohol by any means possible. How has that voice tried to hold you back? Are you willing to release the fears and doubts this voice has instilled in you?

How would you like to see your physical health improve? Do you have a major health concern that you haven't yet been able to crack? Although it may seem unrelated to drinking, alcohol certainly isn't contributing to your body's ability to heal. Perhaps you'd like to see improvements in your energy, sleep, or skin or increase your overall physical fitness. It's difficult to discern how intricately alcohol may be impacting your physical health, so instead of trying to intuit how alcohol has held you back in your physical life, create a vision for what vibrant physical health would look like for you.

Describe the energetic vibration you would like your life to take on as a nondrinker. Imagine the types of people and experiences you'd like to be surrounded by on a daily basis. How far is this from your current reality? Are you willing to believe that you are capable and deserving of living in this vibration most of the time?

Identify some of the areas where your emotional growth may be stunted. Do you believe that you are emotionally capable of dealing with any situation life throws at you? Describe some emotions you find difficult to deal with. Do you believe you are worthy of happiness and capable of having it?

How has alcohol pulled you out of authentic alignment? Do you feel you are being your best self as a drinker? Who do you become when you drink? What about the personality traits you take on after drinking (when hung over)? In everyday life, do you ever feel like you're wearing masks or playing a part? How, if at all, might you be out of authentic alignment in your everyday life?

Where in your life have you been settling for good enough? Where have you stopped short of pursuing your dreams by convincing yourself that you *should* just be happy where you are? Are you willing to believe that you are deserving of more than *good enough*?

By now, you can see that alcohol is not simply a tool for socialization or numbing uncomfortable emotions. Alcohol has, in fact, been keeping you from accessing your potential in subtle ways across many facets of your life. With this new perspective, you are now able to make a vital decision: Will you choose to live an ordinary life dictated by the limitations of alcohol? Or will you choose to step into the extraordinary life of pursuing your fullest potential? We'll discuss these options and opportunities further in the next chapter.

CHAPTER 5

You Weren't Meant for Ordinary

Embracing Your Birthright for More

One of the most—if not *the most*—massive breakthroughs I've ever had came just a few months into my initial break from alcohol. Remember, at that time, I'd not officially determined my long-term plan for me and booze. I was in the shower one day, casually lathering my hair with shampoo when, out of nowhere, I heard a loud, overwhelming message from my Inner Guide: "I see you doing big things in this world," she offered, "but I can't see you doing them with alcohol in the picture." I was completely shaken and overcome with emotion as warm energy rushed through my body. I gasped for air and lowered myself to the shower floor as tears flooded my eyes. I sat there for several minutes, regaining my composure. My Inner Guide had spoken loud and clear, and I couldn't unhear the message. It was in that moment that I knew my relationship with alcohol hadn't just changed; it was over. And although I wasn't quite sure what *big things* were in store for me, I believed with my whole heart that the words of my Inner Guide were true. Right then, I committed to pursuing this new alcohol-free path whole-heartedly.

Even if your Inner Guide hasn't delivered a life-altering message to you as mine did, I believe that she's been whispering to you, quietly and intently reminding you of your potential and encouraging you to stop diluting yourself so that you have the capacity to explore it. No matter if you're a wind-down-at-the-end-of-the-day drinker or an only-on-the-weekends drinker or someone who is currently abstaining and trying to figure out if this change is long term, I believe you were guided to this path for a reason. I trust that deep down you, too, know that you have big work to do and that changing your relationship with alcohol might just be the final piece in the puzzle that is your potential.

WHAT IS POTENTIAL?

There's a huge misconception that realizing your potential has to do with achieving some sort of professional or intellectual goal. While your career and intellectual pursuits are aspects of your potential, metrics and accolades are not the only ways we realize our potential.

I see potential as an inherent ability to become the most authentic, self-expressed, embodied version of yourself. I look at potential on a holistic scale and believe that it can be expressed through your personal fulfillment, emotional capacity, relationship quality, professional success, and spiritual connection. As you'll learn through reading this book, I believe alcohol significantly hinders your ability to perform in these vital life areas, thus keeping you from feeling fulfilled.

I have witnessed firsthand—in my own life and the lives of thousands of clients and students—an unimaginable transformation that occurs in individuals who make the conscious choice to remove alcohol from their lifestyles. I'm not exaggerating when I say that every area of my life changed for the better once alcohol was out of the picture. As an alcohol-free woman, I have an increased appetite for success, a higher threshold for what success looks like, and a greater capacity to go after my vision of success.

No matter what potential means to you, it is your divine responsibility to share your potential with the world. You, my friend, weren't meant for ordinary.

As you begin to unpack your potential, it's important that you have some frames for understanding where you still have space to grow. There are many ways to look at this, but for ease of consumption, I've separated potential into major categories for you to reflect on:

Personal potential: Your passions, hobbies, and recreational goals and dreams. Often, we put our personal goals on hold as we shift from adolescence into adulthood because they're not considered productive. However, I contend that passions and hobbies are some of our most important pursuits. Your dreams and desires are waiting for you; choosing not to make time for them is a direct violation of your potential.

Emotional potential: Your ability to name, feel, communicate about, and self-soothe through your most basic and intense emotions. Most of us were not taught to safely experience and share our emotions, so we struggle with this as adults. The capacity to sit with both positive and negative emotions is essential to your ability to express your potential.

Social potential: Fulfilling your need for vulnerable, reciprocal human connection on the platonic level. Connection and belonging are essential to the human experience. Although alcohol is touted as a social lubricant, drinking dilutes social connection by preventing you from having the energy to be vulnerable.

Romantic potential: The depth of your romantic and sexual relationships. We often use alcohol to cultivate closeness, vulnerability, and arousal in our romantic lives. As in social relationships, alcohol dilutes your ability to connect romantically and sexually and frequently leads to unproductive (or forgotten) conversations and arguments.

Professional potential: Your ability to share your most genius gifts and get paid abundantly to do so. Even high achievers who have found tremendous professional success as drinkers find that sobriety helps them step into new expressions of their professional potential.

Spiritual potential: Your capacity to cultivate a connection with a higher power of your own understanding. It is your ability to tap into your intuition and choose faith over fear. Getting to know your spiritual nature in a way that feels good to you is the ultimate expression of your potential.

YOU WERE MEANT FOR EXTRAORDINARY

On some level, I believe you know you were meant for something extraordinary. You have always known this, but somewhere along the way, you got caught up in the allure of doing ordinary, average, normal things and expecting extraordinary results. I have no doubt that you've accomplished some tremendous things and overcome insurmountable obstacles in this lifetime. Yet I also believe that all of your accomplishments are minor successes in comparison to your full potential.

What would it look like if you were free to become the you that you were always meant to be? What would it look like if you had absolutely nothing holding you back as you embarked on the journey to pursue the most wild and wonderful version of your life? How would your life change if you allowed yourself to shine at your brightest? How much of that light would spill over into the lives of those around you, allowing your family, friends, colleagues, and acquaintances to benefit from your radiance?

I believe that your bravery to explore and express your potential will have a massive positive impact on the world around you. You were meant to live the most extraordinary version of your life that is available. Yet most of us have settled for the ordinary and tried to convince ourselves that we should just be happy with what we have. Yes, by all means, show gratitude for the life you live. But please do not for one more second attempt to convince yourself of the lie that you should be happy where you are, especially if should-ing yourself into complacency has required you to dilute your potential with alcohol because that's *what everyone else is doing*. It may feel arrogant to embrace this concept, but you are not meant to follow the crowd. You are not meant for the ordinary. You are meant for the extraordinary.

This isn't some Pollyanna fantasy I'm trying to sell you on. It is the truth. It is your birthright; you need only to have the bravery to step outside of the ordinary to claim it. How do I know this? Because you have been curious enough to ask existential questions like, Is this all there is? Or, Would my life be better without alcohol? These are not questions that are pondered by someone who is at the peak of their potential. These are questions pondered by someone like you, who has so much more to give and knows, intuitively, that alcohol is keeping you stuck.

unbottle your potential

Going from Ordinary to Extraordinary

Have you received messages or nudges from your Inner Guide? Tune in and connect with the part of your subconscious that has been guiding you toward the path of elective sobriety.

Write down any specific messages, suggestions, gut feelings, or encouragements you've received from your Inner Guide.

What does potential mean to you? Describe what it would look like for you to be living in a full expression of your potential. Consider what life for your future successful self might look like in one to three years. I recommend writing this out as a present-tense story as if you are waking up and going through your day one to three years in the future. Describe this day vividly, and write about how you feel living life in this way. As you put your pen to paper, don't edit what falls onto the page. Remember, if you are creative enough to dream it, you are capable of bringing it to fruition. Often, I find that even the wildest dreams you put on paper in this early stage are only a fraction of what you are capable of. So dream big and know that even your biggest dreams pale in comparison to what the Universe has in store for you.

Do you have a bigger why? Many of my clients are inspired to share bigger whys behind their decision to pursue an alcohol-free lifestyle. Some people have a self-focused why, while others have an other-focused why. Your why could be as broad as feeding your desire to fulfill a bigger dream that you are still uncovering or as specific as showing up as a more present parent for your children.

What is your vision of success in each broad area of potential? Refer to my broad definitions above and spend some time creating a list of some of your goals, dreams, and desires for each of these categories of potential:

- **Personal**
- **Romantic**
- **Emotional**
- **Professional**
- **Social**
- **Spiritual**

I recommend you consider these questions and come back to this chapter as often as necessary as your vision for what's possible for your life continues to expand.

To access online resources and guides to help you connect to your potential, visit amandakuda.com/unbottledresources.

Now that you have a basic understanding of how alcohol has bottled up your brilliance, you're ready to move on to part 2 of this book, Claiming Your Unbottled Life, where I'll help you navigate the everyday challenges of removing alcohol from your life and give you new tools for using your alcohol-free lifestyle as a springboard for fully unbottling your potential.

part two

CLAIMING YOUR UNBOTTLED LIFE

CHAPTER 6

If It's Not Fun without Alcohol, Maybe It's Just Not Fun

Reimagining Your Social Life as a Nondrinker

Alcohol doesn't make things interesting; it makes your
mind stupid so that things that would otherwise have
bored it are suddenly enough to occupy it.

William Porter, *Alcohol Explained*

In the spring of 2017, just five months into my alcohol-free journey, my friend Summer invited me to be her plus-one to a wedding at an all-inclusive resort in Tulum, Mexico. Believe it or not, at thirty-one, I'd never been out of the country, and I knew that Summer would be a fun travel partner who could also be respectful of my decision to abstain, as she was the person who'd introduced me to the concept of Dry January in the first place. Being a savvy traveler, Summer suggested we also take advantage of timing and location and pop over to Havana, Cuba, for a few days after the wedding. To say I was excited would have been an understatement.

By this point, I'd already committed to taking a full six-month break from alcohol. I was just a month away from meeting my goal by the time we arrived in Mexico. I started the trip with my confidence high, and I looked forward to experiencing my trip clear-headed and hangover-free. But my enthusiasm began to dwindle as we stepped onto the resort, where I was immediately offered an umbrella-topped cocktail and found myself surrounded by carefree travelers and the promise of endless free tropical drinks. Suddenly, my confidence turned into doubt and dread.

I started down an anxiety spiral, intricately playing out the worst-case scenarios in my head. I worried I wouldn't be able to relax and fully enjoy my vacation. I felt anxious about being surrounded by strangers, all cutting loose and having the time of their lives at a wedding while I was the sober loser. Immediately, my fear of missing out set in. Everywhere I turned, there was an opportunity to falter on the commitment I'd made to myself.

There was a moment when I thought, You should just make an exception. You've done so well; don't you deserve a reward? After all, you've paid for unlimited drinks; why not relax and have some fun? The idea of wasting money almost sent me over the edge. Then I walked by the resort's poolside bar and took inventory of what "all-inclusive" drinks included. Even the liquors that lined the top shelf of the bar guaranteed nothing but an all-consuming hangover. Out of the corner of my eye, I spotted a juice bar, and that became my saving grace. Instead of spending my week drinking cheap booze and wine, I enjoyed an endless supply of smoothies and juices and felt all the better for it.

I relished the feeling of waking up in paradise, hangover-free. Without the hazy veil of alcohol to cover my senses, I was able to experience every moment of my trip through the eyes of wonder. We hiked through Mayan ruins, snorkeled, and explored whimsical cenotes. We swam with dolphins and manatees and did goofy water aerobics. I remember every epic moment of that trip. Although I thought I might miss out on all the fun by not drinking, I honestly think it was the first time in my adult life I experienced what fun is.

TURN FOMO INTO JOMO

My experience in Mexico is a perfect example of turning the fear of missing out (FOMO) into the *joy* of missing out (JOMO). This skill will become your superpower as an alcohol-free person. Once I became willing to see the world through the eyes of joy rather than fear, my perception and entire experience shifted.

When I consider what I actually missed out on during that trip—free bottom-shelf booze, emotional numbness, and brutal hangovers—I realize that I wasn't missing out on much. **It's ironic that we all tend to psych ourselves out over the fun we'll miss if we're the only ones not drinking. In reality, the only thing we're missing out on is being drunk.**

The simple fact is that I would have missed out on so much more had I chosen to drink on my trip. I would have missed out on the full sensory experience of the ocean air and the epic sunsets. I would have missed out on the acute awareness I had on each and every adventure. Had I been hung over, I would have sulked through the Mayan ruins and nursed an unavoidable headache while swimming in the cenotes. I would have been numb to my emotions and wouldn't have experienced the pure, childlike bliss of swimming with dolphins and having a manatee nuzzle my leg. And, if I'm being brutally honest, I probably would have hurled on the tour bus full of strangers as we whipped through rocky jungle back roads on the way to all of our sightseeing adventures.

What I experienced on my trip was the joy of missing out. I want you to experience this joy, too, because it is nothing short of exceptional. Whether you're navigating the fear of missing out during a vacation or an everyday social event, you can use this five-step method for turning FOMO into JOMO:

Step 1: **Commit to your joy.** The first step for shifting FOMO to JOMO is committing to your joy. When you commit to joy, you are not only committing to experiencing the joy that's available to you in the moment but also the extended pride and joy you will feel each time you conquer an experience sober.

I have never had a client tell me they regretted staying sober at an event, at a social gathering, or on vacation. On the contrary, they've always recounted how confident they felt about staying strong in the face of temptation.

Step 2: **Play the tape forward.** If you've found yourself in a FOMO spiral, take a moment to play the tape forward and get real about what you're missing out on. How do you normally feel after you drink? Sluggish, anxious, regretful, dreadfully hung over? Are these really the experiences you desire?

A great example of playing the tape forward comes from my client Theresa, who told me she often missed the feeling of relaxing and having a glass of wine with her girlfriends or partner. Every few weeks, when the weather was nice or the kids were with a sitter, she'd fantasize about those precious few moments when she'd slip under the spell of alcohol. Yet before I could offer her any coaching and encouragement, Theresa would undoubtedly follow up with a confident affirmation that she'd played the tape forward and was not interested in the consequences that came from that temporary trip into emotional numbness. For Theresa, that feeling was always fleeting and frequently morphed into anger, rage, or anxiety. The nights with her girlfriends turned into blurry memories, and romantic evenings with her partner could quickly shift to bickering. By playing the tape forward, Theresa was able to do the math and remember that the payoff wouldn't be worth the momentary reward.

Admittedly, playing the tape forward can be extremely challenging when faced with the very real fear of missing out on whatever you believe others are experiencing. If you find yourself getting stuck here, move on to step 3.

Step 3: Get clear on what you think you're missing. My client Dianna was plagued by FOMO when she hired me as her coach. Dianna and her family had just moved to their dream home in a new neighborhood and were inundated with friends and family members bringing by fancy bottles of wine to celebrate.

Dianna told me that what she was most afraid of missing out on was the shared experience of having a bottle of wine with her friends. For one, Dianna had coded wine as a sophisticated experience where everyone was discussing vintages, vineyards, and tannins. In addition, Dianna felt herself being jealous of her friends who slowly slipped into another energetic dimension with each sip while she stayed rooted in reality.

For connoisseurs, the thought of missing out on the experience of wine, craft beer, bourbon, or your favorite drink of choice can feel defeating. I can see the temptation behind paying respect to the craft of fermentation, brewing, and distilling. I mean no disrespect to the masters of these fields. If I'm being honest, I still don't have a foolproof argument for those who identify as connoisseurs of any type. And yet, I say this lovingly: I haven't met a single sober-curious person who can honestly tell me they sit around with their friends and wax philosophical about the craft of making alcohol. I've even had clients who are sommeliers or otherwise in the alcohol industry tell me they rarely get into a truly intelligent discussion about wine.

When I ask my clients to describe the shared experience with me, they confess that the conversations are typically some version of "Try this expensive wine; it tastes good." Therefore, I always challenge them with the uncomfortable question: Couldn't your shared experience have been just as meaningful, and much more memorable, if you had enjoyed, say, a piece of decadent cake from a talented baker? Admittedly, most of my clients become uncomfortably silent when I ask this question. The harsh reality is that the thing you most miss out on when you choose not to drink is the momentary bliss of getting tipsy or drunk.

Step 4: **Nurture your inner child.** Deep down, most of us are self-conscious adolescents living in adult bodies, and our most basic desire is to fit in. It's imperative that you nurture this inner adolescent and commit to living to your full potential as an individuated, self-expressed, mature adult.

When I stopped drinking, there was nothing that I secretly feared more than reverting to the gawky, awkward teenage girl I'd tried to leave behind all those years ago. I'd done my best to mask her insecurities by adopting my Party Girl persona, but on the inside, seventeen-year-old me was still running the show. Instead of being angry with her or ashamed, I chose to do what I hadn't had the skills for all those years ago: I chose to love and nurture her. When I did, I realized that most of my lingering FOMO came from her.

Even many of my clients who didn't begin drinking until well into adulthood share that they did so to fit in with their peers, colleagues, and romantic partners. Wherever your FOMO stems from, I encourage you to work on loving and nurturing the part of you that is afraid of being rejected or excluded.

To begin, make this your mantra: "I am deserving and capable of having fun."

*To dive deeper, visit the resources webpage for this book at amandakuda
.com/unbottledresources to complete my Fighting FOMO tapping se-
quence using the Emotional Freedom Technique.*

Step 5: See through the eyes of joy. I am always in awe of how
much joy and beauty I can experience now that I'm alcohol-free.
It's as if I'm Dorothy in *The Wizard of Oz*, finally seeing the world
in Technicolor for the first time. As a sober woman, my senses
are now heightened to the world around me. Tapping into those
senses is a great way to experience more joy.

Early on in my sobriety, I not only made the commitment to
see through the eyes of joy but also to smell, hear, touch, and
taste through joy as well. In every experience, I challenge myself to lean into my senses and fully embrace the experience
available to me. Each time, I am astounded by how beautiful
and miraculous the world around me is.

As I write this chapter, I'm overlooking the beautiful jungle of
Costa Rica. I can see ornery monkeys climbing through the trees
just outside my window. I hear the uplifting sounds of birds
chirping and distant waves crashing at the ocean shore. I feel the
warmth of the sun and smell the delicious food that my new
friend, Chef Lindell, is generously preparing for me. In just a few
hours, I'll enjoy the epic meal he has poured his soul into cook-
ing. This is more memorable and precious than any fleeting experience I've had from a fancy glass of wine.

It might sound as if I'm seeing the world through rose-colored
glasses, and if I am, so be it because it's pretty damn fantastic. By
choosing to see through the eyes of joy, I'm constantly surrounded
by beauty. What's more, I've created a life where I get to experience it fully. This moment is not an anomaly. I'm frequently filled
with gratitude and moved to tears because *this* version of my life
is so miraculous.

If you're having trouble tapping into joy, take a moment to
complete the following Five Senses Meditation. If you're able,

consider stepping outside or looking out your window. If not, you can close your eyes and envision yourself in your favorite place in nature.

Five Senses Meditation

Come into a comfortable seated position, rolling your shoulders back and releasing any tension that's built up in your body.

With your eyes open, begin to slow your breath, breathing in through your nose for four counts, holding for four counts, exhaling through your nose for four counts, and holding for another four counts at the bottom.

Continue this breath cycle throughout this meditation.

Keeping your head still, slowly begin to shift your gaze, observing your surroundings. Direct your visual focus to something that brings you delight. Take a moment to appreciate and enjoy the sight.

Now move your attention slowly to your other senses.

As you inhale through your nose, notice what smells are present in the air.

Notice any sensations you feel in your body. Feel your seat beneath you or perhaps the ground. If you're able, place your hands and feet on the earth, observing the texture and temperature.

Now tune in to the sounds that are around you. Pinpoint a sound to focus on. Can you find enjoyment in listening?

As you look around, notice something nearby you might be able to taste. Center in on the sensations of taste.

Allow yourself to find joy and delight in each sensory experience. Can you find a sense of lightheartedness and gratitude for your current surroundings? Sit for a moment more and experience the joy of being present in the moment.

When you're ready, gently begin to move around and come back to the room, bringing the experience of joy with you.

You can access a recording of this guided meditation at amandakuda .com/unbottledresources.

YOU'RE SOBER, NOT BORING

Back in Mexico, I was flying high by the time the night of the wedding rolled around. I was blissed-out on adventures and sunshine, but as soon as cocktail hour hit, my confidence took a turn. As an adult, I'd never been to a wedding sober. I barely knew any of the other guests, and the ones I did know were all old business school friends of the bride. I was no stranger to this particular business school crowd and knew they were notorious for tying one on. The closer we got to dinnertime, the more anxious I became about the evening festivities. As someone who'd always identified as the life of the party, I was in my head about the possibility that I'd now come off as shy and boring.

In that moment, I made a commitment to myself: just because I was sober didn't mean I had to be boring. Since I love to dance, I committed to proving to myself that I could have fun at a wedding without taking advantage of the open bar. Luckily, the bride's family were big dancers and there was no lack of opportunity to hit the dance floor. Now, years later, I'll run into the bride, and she'll gush about how much fun I was at her wedding. Sure enough, her wedding photos included many images of me smiling and dancing the night away.

Just because you're sober doesn't mean you are boring. Taking a break from alcohol is not the equivalent of taking a break from fun. Life is fun. *You* are fun and able to *have* fun without the support of alcohol to loosen you up. If you're skeptical, I invite you to remember a few moments in your childhood when you were having fun. What were you doing? Were you playing make-believe, dancing, singing, or riding a bicycle downhill? Maybe you found your fun exploring or learning or reading a book. Even if you had a less than ideal childhood, I'm willing to bet you can remember one moment when you were having fun. I will not, for one single second, believe that you, my dear reader, are completely boring and incapable of having fun without alcohol.

Somewhere along the way, many of us picked up a small-minded yet potent idea that we needed to be tipsy to have fun or be fun. In my coaching business, I have spreadsheets full of data from thousands of students who list their number-one fear of sobriety as becoming a social recluse because they can no longer participate in "fun" activities. If that sounds like you, here are five rules to help you find your fun:

Rule 1: Be willing to have fun. My positive experience in Mexico was reliant on one major decision: I became willing to have fun. I made the conscious decision that I would *try* to have fun. This meant leaning into an experience even though I wasn't entirely sure if I would enjoy it without alcohol versus choosing to be a stick-in-the-mud, sulking because I was not drinking while everyone else was. If you want to have fun, you have to be willing to *try*. There will inevitably be activities that you try your hand at and discover they're not fun for you; that's okay. We'll discuss this further with rule 3, but suffice to say that the only way you'll know if something is actually fun or not is if you are willing to explore life with an open mind.

Rule 2: Reimagine fun. Take a moment to make a list of activities you found fun as a child and adolescent. These might be activities that lit you up or things you were able to get lost in for hours. When did you stop doing them, and why? You might have lost touch with fun because you outgrew an activity or believed the lie that something wasn't worth your time if it wasn't productive or monetizable. You might have even abandoned your fun because you were made to feel shame around your interest. Maybe you had a teacher or parent who criticized your skill or a peer who made fun of you. Whatever the case, I'm willing to bet that there are fun activities that you stopped allowing yourself to enjoy at one point or another.

I've always been a dancer. As a little girl, I begged to be put in dance classes. (I mentioned earlier that my mom often cleaned my dance teacher's house to pay for my lessons.) I'll never forget the day the owner of our studio called me out in front of my entire dance class to ask when my parents planned to pay our outstanding bill for my shoes and costumes. I was sixteen and at the height of my teenage insecurity. I was humiliated and heartbroken. It's no coincidence that a few months later I decided to quit dance and devote my time to theater classes instead.

When I left for college, I chose a university that offered a dance major, secretly hoping to revisit my passion. I took two years of collegiate-level dance classes before convincing myself that dance wasn't a lucrative career. It took me nearly a decade to revisit my love for dance—not including, of course, my innumerable nights drunkenly spent on the dance floor during my Party Girl days. It wasn't until after I quit drinking that I had the time and energy to revisit dance. Today, I regularly participate in a women's hip-hop dance class, and these are the days I have the most fun. I almost always leave with a new friend, and I spend hours buzzing and recounting the routines in my home. Dancing is one of my outlets for fun, and I encourage you to find yours, too.

Today, make a commitment to doing something you used to find fun but have abandoned. Bring the commitment to life by enrolling in a class, scheduling a lesson, or doing whatever you need to do to hold yourself accountable. Add your fun event to your calendar, and be sure to post about it and tag me on Instagram (I'm @amandakuda, by the way) so I can share in the fun with you!

Rule 3: **If it's not fun without alcohol, maybe it's just not fun.** When I first stopped drinking, I did a major doozy to my self-confidence by trying to convince myself that it was me who was not fun. When I thrust myself back into social environments like happy hour, boozy brunch, and Sunday Funday without the assistance of alcohol, I told myself the lie that I was the problem.

I tried my best to maintain a similar social calendar in a desperate attempt not to become a social recluse, only to find these events were no longer enough to hold my attention. I learned I didn't have the tolerance for shouting over music in loud bars, elbowing my way through packed clubs, or engaging in small talk and gossip with my tipsy friends. I left most social activities feeling disconnected because I wasn't able to have any semblance of a meaningful conversation with my friends. When I started looking around, I made the harsh realization: **if it's not fun without alcohol, maybe it's just not fun.**

At first, this hypothesis felt a little unsettling because I wasn't quite sure what I was supposed to do for fun if the things I used to do for fun were now a total snooze.

In chapter 8, I'll teach you new ways to connect with your friends that don't require you to tolerate unbearable experiences, but I also want to empower you to test the waters and confirm this theory for yourself. You might be surprised to find that there are activities that you do still enjoy or can enjoy with some conscious boundaries (which we'll discuss in rule 5).

Rule 4: **Feel into your nervous system.** As a nondrinker, you may begin to realize that the activities you used to enjoy are not only boring but utterly exhausting. Without alcohol to numb your senses, you may find yourself feeling overwhelmed and over-stimulated in rowdy social environments.

Many of my clients who identify as super social are actually empaths, introverts, and other deep-feeler types who uncon-sciously use alcohol as a way to numb their nervous system's re-action to overstimulation. As drinkers, we're able to shut off or quiet our body's reaction to a variety of stimuli such as noise and crowds. This is enough to *convince* ourselves that we enjoy the environment when, in fact, we are only turning off the part of our brain that alerts us that the environment or situation is a lot for us to handle.

If you find yourself feeling easily overwhelmed or energetically drained by social environments that you used to think were ex-hilarating, it's important to consider that this may be your nervous system reacting to overstimulation. If so, it's vital that you learn to honor your limits and set boundaries around when and why you're willing to thrust yourself into these types of environments.

Rule 5: **Set new boundaries.** Once you've become clear on what feels fun for you and what doesn't, it's time to begin setting and enforcing new boundaries for yourself. For instance, I still enjoy getting together with my old crew of friends from time to time, but I've realized that my time is more enjoyable if I set certain boundaries for myself.

To begin, I'm a fan of going to potentially boozy social events early so I can spend more time with people before their eyes be-gin to glaze over from drinking. I always give myself permission to go to a social event and leave early, even if everyone else seems to be having the time of their lives. In these situations, I optimize my time for connection. If I feel my contemporaries have moved into an energetic space where we're no longer able to meaning-fully connect on a similar level, it's time for me to go. If you feel yourself dipping back into a little FOMO over leaving a party early, let me assure you I cannot name a single time when I've missed something important by leaving the party. Typically, I even end up serving as a sober driver for a grateful friend who is also ready to leave the party. This is a win-win because I feel more confident about leaving if someone else is ready to leave, too, and I get the satisfaction of helping out a friend.

Believe it or not, you also have full permission to skip social events entirely. I know, it was a wild concept for me at first, too. But here's the deal: if you feel completely stressed or unenthused about going to a party or event, don't go. Unless it's an important life event or a work function that you absolutely *must* attend, just don't go. It's as simple as that.

I can't tell you how many hours I've gained and how much energy I've saved by choosing not to go to the party . . . or the happy hour . . . or the *whatever* because I was able to admit that it genuinely didn't sound fun. Now I can devote these hours to doing things I actually find fun and pursuing my potential.

A hidden bonus to following these rules is that when you're having fun, your confidence and creativity automatically grow. As a drinker, I constantly felt lackluster and uninspired. As an alcohol-free woman, I find that I'm frequently inspired by my surroundings and motivated by the activities I choose to invest my time in. Making a commitment to joy and true fun will have tremendous payoffs that you can't even begin to imagine yet.

MAKE PEACE WITH BOREDOM

As you shift your social priorities and begin to step more fully into pursuing your potential, there will inevitably be times when you experience boredom. There will be nights and weekends when you find yourself with no plans, and that's okay. This time is important—vital, even—for your growth. You see, we tend to avoid boredom by overfilling our social calendars, drinking, scrolling, and bingeing TV. Although there is nothing wrong with checking out from time to time, we live in a world where many of us have little tolerance for boredom because it is in boredom that we are confronted with sitting with our emotions.

In the next chapter, I'm going to guide you to find the beauty in boredom, as you can use it as a powerful space to embrace your emotions. I believe our emotions hold massive wisdom and can unlock powerful doors to pursuing our potential. The more competent and confident we become with sitting with our emotions, the more capable we are of stepping into our best lives.

CHAPTER 7

Embracing Your Emotions

*Learning to Ride the Highs and Lows of Life
with Ease, Grace, and Confidence*

I did not know that I was supposed to feel *everything*.
I thought I was supposed to feel *happy*.

Glennon Doyle, *Untamed*

Most of us are afraid to feel through and sit with our emotions. Our most intense emotions, from the depths of grief and sorrow to the highs of joy and bliss, can feel overwhelming in a world where it's unlikely that you were ever given the tools, encouragement, or permission to demonstrate and openly feel into your vast emotional range. Ill-equipped to deal with such emotions, it's common to turn to a cocktail or a night out on the town to numb, dull, or attempt to forget the enormity of your internal experience.

Take, for example, my client Danielle. From a young age, Danielle was encouraged to mask her emotions and show up as a mature child. When she should have been playing with dolls and toys, Danielle was caring for her sisters and walking on eggshells around her super strict father and narcissistic mother. Danielle was empathic and emotional but didn't have role models who showed her how to embrace her big feelings. Rather, both of Danielle's parents encouraged her to put on a strong face. As a result, Danielle felt overwhelmed anytime intense emotions would build up. Although she didn't drink often, Danielle would hit her emotional limit every few weeks and numb out with several cocktails or glasses of wine. The next day, Danielle reported that her overwhelm and anxiety were typically worse than the day before. When we began working together, she desperately wanted the tools and confidence to feel through her emotions instead of using alcohol to self-medicate.

You might also resonate with my client Nikki, who grew up in a household where cynical family members were always waiting for the other shoe to drop. Nikki was never given the impression that happiness was her birthright, and as a result, she had a sneaky way of self-sabotaging every time life started getting *too good*. Just after Nikki and I began working together, she called to report that she'd had a nasty run-in with alcohol on the brink of an extremely high moment in her life. Although she intended to have a drink as a means of celebration, Nikki's unconscious urge to subdue the good feeling caused her to overdo it. Instead of riding the high of her success, Nikki ended up embarrassing herself in front of friends and starting a petty argument with her partner. Sadly, her happy moment was overshadowed by the shame she felt over her drunken behavior.

On some level, we all drink to avoid dealing with uncomfortable or impermissible emotions. Those emotions might range from shyness and anxiety to boredom and overwhelm, anger, and rage. They might even include excitement and euphoria. When we don't know how to deal with emotions, our quickest fix is to dilute them with alcohol.

Throughout this chapter, we'll dive into understanding and embracing your emotions so that you can have the knowledge and tools you need to proudly experience the emotional highs and lows that come along with this experience that is life.

EMOTIONAL PROCESSING 101

In a perfect world, we would have been taught that our emotions are sacred and that it is safe to feel them. Ideally, we all would have been raised in environments that encouraged us to cope with our emotions, communicate our feelings, and self-soothe during difficult times. Realistically, most of us grew up in imperfect emotional environments, and the tools we were given to process our emotional experience of the world were mediocre at best. As children, we mirror how our parents experience various emotional states, using their behaviors as a template for our own. Most of us didn't have parents who were strong in this area, so in turn, we struggle to cope with overwhelming emotions and experiences.

Of course, our parents were doing the best they could, but they often sent us mixed signals by behaving one way and demanding that we behave another. If you had parents whose actions and words were incongruent, expressing emotions might feel confusing for you as an adult. For example, you may have had parents who had angry outbursts but sent you to your room if you displayed your own anger or rage. This may have made your intense emotions seem impermissible and wrong. Therefore, as an adult, you may have difficulty holding space for similar emotions.

Likewise, you may have grown up in a family where emotions such as sadness were not honored. Perhaps your parents hid their tears or discouraged you from crying when you were upset. If this is the case, you may struggle to emote through tears or feel overwhelmed with vulnerability when crying. I've encountered very few clients who grew up in households where emotions were talked about and celebrated.

If your emotions weren't validated and expressed in healthy ways as a child, it can only be expected that you'd experience trouble managing emotions in your teens and twenties as you in-dividuate from your family of origin and become responsible for your own emotional experiences. Incidentally, this is often the same time we are introduced to alcohol as an emotional crutch. We receive messages from peers, media, and mentors that alcohol is an acceptable coping mechanism. So rather than learning effec-tive coping tools, we cheat our way through emotional experiences such as stress, grief, and heartache with a cocktail at our side.

Ironically, negative or intense emotions aren't the only ones we have trouble expressing. It's also possible that you grew up in a family unit where joy was seen as imprudent. I've worked with clients who grew up in households where they were told to settle down if they were too joyous or were advised to always be on guard. These experiences can cause us to feel unsafe when we encounter extreme positive emotions as adults.

We also learn that alcohol can be used as a tool to enhance our positive emotional experiences. Just as we turn to alcohol to drown our sorrows, we imbibe to elevate our joy. If you look at the use case for alcohol more closely, it's difficult not to become concerned. Is it practical to believe that a single substance can be responsible for both calming our misery and elevating our joy? Yet this is the power we've given to alcohol. We've made it an emotional cure-all in our lives. All the while, we've been cheat-ing ourselves of the opportunity to learn to be with our emo-tions. For those who have come to rely on alcohol as an emotional anesthetic, the thought of taking booze out of the equation might feel extremely confronting.

Emotional Trauma and Mental Health

Quite often, alcohol is used—either passively or actively—to escape traumatic memories and overwhelming mental illnesses. Although numbing with alcohol is not a productive long-term strategy, it can often feel like the only tool we have to keep our nervous system safe. In this sense, we use drinking to protect ourselves from accessing emotions we are not quite yet ready to process. If this was your path, please be gentle with yourself and know that you were doing your best to cope with insurmountable circumstances in your life.

Even if you have experienced emotional trauma or mental illness, it remains that you are an extremely powerful and intuitive emotional being. If you have been called to pursue an alcohol-free lifestyle, I trust that your Inner Guide knows you are coming to a place where you are emotionally able to cope with or process all that you have been using alcohol to avoid. If you feel you have used alcohol to block the memory of a trauma or make a mental illness seem more manageable, I encourage you to seek therapeutic support as part of your journey to go alcohol-free.

SHOWING UP FOR EMOTIONAL EXPERIENCES

Emotional wellness relies on our willingness to become aware of our emotions, have intelligence about those emotions, and develop the skill to sit with and feel through our emotions. Because drinking can stunt your emotional growth in this area, exploring your emotional potential will likely feel awkward and overwhelming at first.

Remember: You are a tremendously powerful being, and you do not need anything outside yourself to perform your basic human functions, such as feeling. You are a full-spectrum individual gifted with the extraordinary ability to experience an unlimited range of emotions. You would not have been given the ability to feel these emotions if you were not capable and deserving of them.

Understanding this, believing this, and taking action to increase your capacity to experience emotions at both ends of the emotional spectrum is one of the keys to a wholehearted life. If you're going to unbottle your potential, it is important that you first acknowledge where your emotional growth has been stunted by drinking and begin to exercise your ability to feel those emotions so that they are less foreign in your body.

Unbottling your emotional potential is the gateway to expressing your potential in each of the other areas we will discuss in this section. Without embracing your capacity to feel, you will be ill-equipped to deal with the vulnerable moments—both negative and positive—that are bound to occur as you expand and grow.

Throughout the rest of this chapter, I'll offer you my most basic first steps for increasing your capacity for both lower-vibe and higher-vibe emotions so that you can begin to feel safe and competent holding space for your own emotional experiences.

Through implementing these practices—along with a lot of therapy, learning, and coaching—I've transformed from someone whose default emotional states included apathy and anxiety into a young woman who operates primarily from a place of joy and inner peace. Although my life is still full of challenges that cause me to frequently veer into negativity, stress, and anxiety, the work I have done has left me with a level of emotional resilience that allows me to quickly navigate back to my default state of peace.

INCREASING YOUR CAPACITY FOR LOWER-VIBE EMOTIONS

One of the most common uses for alcohol is to numb out or avoid our lower-vibe emotions. It's the glass of wine at the end of a long day to wind down or shut off your thoughts. It's the cocktail after a particularly stressful life event. It's drowning your sorrows after a loss or heartbreak.

You know by now that alcohol doesn't get rid of the troubles in your life or the troublesome feelings. Rather, it delays your lower-vibe emotions before magnifying them. You've surely felt the uncomfortable and common hangover anxiety after a night of drinking away your woes. This is essentially your nervous system having a little freak-out that you haven't dealt with the root problem and are now too energetically depleted to do so.

Drinking to avoid lower-vibe emotions is like cleaning your room by shoving filthy clothes and dirty dishes under the bed. Hiding the mess doesn't make it go away. Rather, it causes the mess to build and build until it either spills over or starts to stink so badly it draws attention to itself. Your emotions are no different. If you choose to repress them by refusing to sort through them as they come up, they'll eventually explode or become overwhelmingly distracting.

Unprocessed emotions are the root of disease, depression, and low self-worth. When you choose to avoid an emotion rather than process or feel it, you send your subconscious the message that you are incapable of feeling and owning the emotion. This is not true. Some emotions will be uncomfortable and overwhelming, but the more you can increase your capacity for feeling through a tough emotion, the more emotionally resilient you will become and the more your self-worth will grow.

Increase Your Emotional Awareness

The first step to cultivating emotional awareness is to become an expert at naming your emotions and identifying their intensity. For this exercise, I like to start with a tool called the emotion wheel. *(Find a copy of the emotion wheel on the resources webpage for this book: amandakuda.com/unbottledresources.)* The wheel has core emotions written in the center and expands to two additional levels with more specific expressions of these emotions. Begin by choosing your base emotion in the center of the wheel, and expand your emotional awareness by choosing secondary and tertiary related emotions on the wheel until you've landed on the most specific description of the emotion you are experiencing. Now rate the intensity at which you're experiencing that emotion on a scale of zero to ten.

For example, if you're feeling the core emotion of anger, locate anger on the wheel and then choose the secondary emotion. Perhaps it's envy. From there, decipher the tertiary or most specific experience of anger. Let's say you identify it as hatred. Now rate how intense that hatred is. For example, you may be feeling hatred at a seven-out-of-ten level.

Begin practicing this with your most intense emotions so that you can become more proficient at recognizing, naming, and communicating your feelings internally.

Learn to WAIT

Once you've identified your emotions and their intensity, you're ready to practice sitting with your emotions. To practice this skill, I often give my clients an exercise using the acronym WAIT, which stands for What Am I Thinking? It is a two-part exercise to use when you feel an uncomfortable emotion start to pop up, particularly if this is an emotion that causes you to want to numb out.

The first part of the WAIT exercise is to recognize when you're feeling an intense emotion that threatens to derail your nervous system or even triggers you to drink. Once you've noticed the presence of an uncomfortable emotion, commit to waiting literally twenty-five to thirty minutes to give yourself some time to sit with the discomfort of the emotion. During this time, you'll remove yourself from the triggering or stressful situation and complete the rest of the exercise.

The second part of this exercise is to journal on the WAIT prompt by asking, What am I thinking? This is a brain-dump journaling exercise designed to allow you to release all the thoughts that are likely rolling around chaotically in your mind. If asking, What am I thinking? is not enough, you could start your free writing with a prompt, such as "The story I'm telling myself is . . ." Feel free to use any prompt that gets you going.

Once you have identified your most specific feeling and its intensity, write and complete this sentence: "I am feeling [insert the most specific emotion or emotions here], but I am willing to feel differently." Now you can move on to one or more of the self-soothing exercises below.

Start Self-Soothing

Learning to self-soothe and cope with our emotions rather than numbing or ignoring them is an essential practice for emotional resilience. Here are my favorite practices that you can choose from to self-soothe.

Hot Pen Journaling

One of the most practical ways to release intense emotions is to write them down. I love using what I call the hot pen technique when working through a tough emotion. When using this technique, you allow your heated emotions to flow from pen onto paper. If you're feeling a particular emotion but not quite calm enough to practice the more structured WAIT exercise I described before, try hot pen journaling.

Here's how it works: Find a quiet place and sit down with no time limit or restrictions. Once your pen hits the paper, don't stop until you've gotten out everything you need to say. Write fervently and aggressively. Let it be messy. Hot pen journaling is not intended to be legible or eloquent. It can be littered with curse words and angry scribbles. This process is helpful for releasing emotions you do not yet feel safe or regulated enough to share with others.

I find hot pen journaling can be a great way to create a messy first draft for a difficult, emotional conversation. My clients who hot pen journal in response to someone or something that has aggravated them report that they can frequently respond from a more levelheaded place versus reacting in the moment.

Primal Experiencing

Your lower-vibe emotions—such as rage, anger, and frustration—are sacred and deserve to be honored, felt, and experienced. Yet because these emotions are culturally perceived as unsavory, we often seek to hide or bury our intense emotions. Rather than hold in your rage and anger, I encourage you to allow them to physically move through your body with a good old-fashioned, primal temper tantrum.

When you feel an intense, lower-vibe emotion coming on, send yourself to your bedroom and let it out. Lie on your bed and flail and scream. Beat a pillow. Cry. Shake your limbs and allow the energy to move through your body. The physical expression of these emotions can be tremendously healing.

Havening

Havening is an exercise that my friend and teacher Anand shared with me a few years back. This self-soothing exercise can be utilized anytime, anyplace to quickly diffuse the intensity of an emotion or recover after any sort of emotional dysregulation.

To begin, rate the intensity of the emotion you are feeling on a scale from zero to ten (ten being the greatest). It's important that you rate your emotions before performing exercises to gain an understanding of how helpful the exercise is in shifting your energetic state. Do not skip this step.

Now sit in a comfortable position and cross your arms so that your hands touch opposite shoulders as if you're hugging yourself. Breathe slowly and deeply in and out through your nose.

Next, slowly stroke down your arms, moving both hands in unison. Stroke from your shoulders, to your biceps, to your elbows, to your forearms, and to your wrists before letting go and returning to the starting position at your shoulders. Complete this caressing movement twenty times. Finish this exercise by re-rating the intensity of your emotion on a scale from zero to ten.

Bilateral Stimulation

I learned this technique from hypnotherapist and founder of the Center for Integrative Hypnosis Melissa Tiers, who taught it as an effective way to bring down the intensity of an anxious episode. This exercise is easiest if you have a small object, such as a water bottle, but you can complete it just as effectively using only your hands by mimicking the movement I'll describe.

Begin by rating the intensity of the anxious feeling on a scale from zero to ten. Next, pick up your object and pass it back and forth from one hand to the other, making sure you cross the center line of your body with each pass. You'll only need to do this exercise for about a minute (sometimes less) to experience relief.

Once you feel your body settle in (known as downregulation), you can conclude the exercise and rerate your emotion.

You can find video tutorials and complementary handouts for these exercises on the resources webpage for this book: amandakuda .com/unbottledresources.

Pray for Support

The metaphysical text *A Course in Miracles* says that prayer is the medium of miracles. The Course also teaches that a miracle is a shift in perception from fear to love. So anytime you find yourself in a fearful, negative, or low-vibe thought pattern or emotion, prayer can be a powerful solution for change.

Even if you don't consider yourself a particularly spiritual person or you're just getting started on your spiritual journey, there are always available solutions that are outside of your physical line of sight. As I have grown stronger in my spiritual practice, I've frequently turned to prayer to support me in situations that seem out of my control or to help me heal an emotion that feels nearly too overwhelming to hold. As my practice has progressed, I'm always amazed at how quickly these shifts in perception become available to me once I call on the Universe for support in reorganizing my thoughts.

It's important to remember that miracles are always available to you; all that is required is your willingness to ask for support. This is because the Universe must honor your free will. If you are intent on solving a problem on your own, the Universe must respect your desire. In other words, the Universe is not in the business of providing unsolicited solutions. Although the Universe is likely to drop hints, engaging in prayer is your way to actively solicit help.

No matter how superficial or seemingly insurmountable the issue is that you are dealing with, I encourage you to pray for support. The Course states that there is no difficulty in the order of miracles, which means that there is no problem—large or small—for which a miracle is not readily available.

If you're just getting started in a prayer practice, it might be helpful to have a few template prayers to get you started. You can use the templates below, filling in the blank spaces with the appropriate information and modifying them as you see fit.

Prayer for Transforming Intense Emotions

Dear Universe,

*I am in emotional pain and unsure how to find my way out
of it on my own. I feel [insert your most intense emotion],
and it does not feel good. I am ready to feel differently.
I need a miracle.*

*I invite you in to help me shift this energy and see a clear
path forward. Please guide me to transform this
emotion so I can see past the intensity and begin healing.
Thank you for supporting me in this healing.
I trust I am now being guided.*

And so it is.

Prayer for Releasing Intense Emotions toward Another

Dear Universe,

*I am feeling [insert your most intense emotion] toward
[insert person's name]. This feeling does not feel good, and
I am ready to feel differently. Please help me release this [restate
the emotion] and see [name] through the lens of innocence
and love. Thank you for helping me shift this negative
emotion and find a path forward.*

And so it is.

Increasing your capacity to hold lower-vibe emotions is a practice, and as you practice and strengthen your skills, you'll find the things that used to shake you up fail to get a rise out of you at the same level they used to. When you do inevitably get shaken up, you'll have the tools to diffuse the intensity of the emotion rather than letting it fester in your body.

Checking In versus Checking Out

Emotional resilience is a practice. The more frequently you can show up for micro-stressors and inconveniences, the more resilient you'll be when bigger life challenges show up. As you work to increase your capacity for low-vibe emotions, be aware of the common tendency to check out with easy-access numbing activities, such as scrolling or swiping on your phone, bingeing on TV, or emotional eating. Each of these activities is a small way to avoid being with our big feelings. You might also transfer your stress to seemingly positive activities, such as obsessively cleaning, exercising, or thrusting yourself into your work or a new hobby. While having outlets where you can safely "check out" is important, be sure you're frequently "checking in" to create ample space to feel and process your emotions.

INCREASING YOUR CAPACITY FOR HIGH-VIBE EMOTIONS

Joy is your intended default state. You are meant to operate from a place of true happiness and peace. This might sound like a fairy tale, but I believe it is true and available to you.

At one point or another, you've probably used alcohol to numb or delay dark, troubling emotions. What you may not have realized is that numbing dark emotions also minimizes your ability to experience light, happy emotions. Or, as Brené Brown puts it, "Numb the dark and you numb the light." As you recalibrate your emotional capacity, it is *your responsibility* to optimize for the high-vibe emotional states that have become foreign in your body.

You've also most likely used alcohol to amplify high-vibe emotions in times of celebration. While this might feel like it increases the good feeling, celebrating with alcohol is a very sneaky way to avoid fully feeling the good, triumphant feelings that accompany celebration.

Outwardly, it can look like we're rocking the high-vibe game when we drink during good times. However, indulging in a champagne toast, shot, or cocktail to celebrate is primarily performative and can cause you to bypass the full internalization of the high-vibe emotion. If this is completely counterintuitive to what you've been taught, stick with me as I explain.

Drinking dulls and delays your capacity to experience emotions. So while you might think you're drinking to extend the good feeling of a win, you're freezing it in time . . . and not in a good way. Because alcohol is a depressant, it quickly brings you down from the good feeling, meaning the height of your happiness over any win is limited to the moment you take a sip.

You are not only depriving yourself of the full experience of the high-vibe emotion but also subconsciously telling your body, This is as good as you deserve to feel. When I dig in with my private coaching clients, they frequently admit they are uncomfortable holding space for and expressing good feelings. They feel like drinking allows them to cut loose and gives them an excuse to outwardly beam and not feel like they're gloating.

Here's the truth: You deserve to feel good. You deserve to experience big, beautiful emotions and to share that experience with others. Sharing your higher-vibe emotions is not gloating or gross. In fact, your demonstration of how to gracefully experience higher-vibe emotions can be expansive to others who struggle with doing the same.

If experiencing and displaying positive emotions does not come naturally to you, we'll want to work on your capacity to recognize this tendency and then take micro-actions to retrain yourself to hold space for these emotions. Even if you do think you're pretty good at the positive emotion thing, I challenge you to try these practices to magnify your good-feeling emotions even more.

Ultimately, I want you to experience what my client Maria noticed after a few months of being alcohol-free. Maria shared, "There are moments, more often than not, where I'm consumed with laughter. It's like this part of my brain was anesthetized and now I'm experiencing joy again."

This level of unfettered joy is absolutely available to you, too, should you choose to recognize where you've been avoiding high-vibe emotions and consciously begin increasing your capacity for them.

Let's look at a couple of common ways we shrug off high-vibe emotions so that you can identify any tendencies you have. You might be surprised at some of the tiny ways you've been avoiding joy. Don't worry; once you become aware of your patterns, they become easier to change.

Avoiding Higher-Vibe Emotions

When onboarding clients and students, I always ask them questions to help me understand how comfortable they are with being happy. Surprisingly, even though happiness is the feeling we all desire, we also have sneaky ways of avoiding happiness. Here are some of the most common ways in which we avoid higher-vibe emotions:

- Deflecting compliments

- Hiding our excitement for fear of seeming arrogant

- Downplaying our success for fear of making others jealous

- Not allowing ourselves to get too excited for fear that we'll jinx the result

- Being on high alert or waiting for the other shoe to drop

If this sounds like you, you're not alone. Our life experiences and cultural upbringing can make it feel safest to be cautious, be reserved, and always see the glass as half-empty. In this sense, it might just be that part of your relationship with alcohol is a sneaky attempt to downplay positive emotions because they do not feel safe to you. Luckily, our human capacity to learn new ways of being is quite magnificent. Here are a few simple exercises to help you increase your capacity for higher-vibe emotions.

Receiving Compliments with Ease and Grace

I love words of affirmation, but anytime someone compliments me, I tend to quickly deflect it by making a self-deprecating comment, shrugging it off, or reciprocating with a compliment in return. Even though I crave affirmation, it's difficult allowing the attention to be on me. I subconsciously worry that others will think I'm egotistical if I bask in kind words. Here are some examples of what it looks like to deflect a compliment . . .

They Say:	You Say:
Wow, I love your outfit.	Thanks, I've had it forever; I got it on sale.
You did a great job on that presentation.	Oh, thank you, but I feel like I messed up on the third slide.
You have such a lovely singing voice.	Well, I'm no Mariah Carey, but thank you.
You look so beautiful today.	Oh, stop. I wish I had your body; you always look so great.

Essentially, deflecting a compliment is anything other than gracefully and humbly saying "Thank you." Women, especially, tend to deflect compliments outwardly in the name of humility. Inwardly, we deflect them because we fear we are undeserving or our brilliance might make others jealous and uncomfortable.

Take, for example, my client Nell, whose new boss had been singing her praises for weeks, proclaiming what a rock star she was in her new role. Nell would typically deflect the compliment with self-deprecating humor or by offering some self-criticism. Nell confessed to me that she was afraid both that she wouldn't be able to live up to the nature of the compliment and that her colleagues would think she was a teacher's pet if she excelled too much. On receiving her most recent compliment, Nell told me she sat silently, aware of her tendency to deflect but unsure what to do instead.

The answer is simple. If you, too, have been in the habit of deflecting compliments, I invite you to put this into practice as well. First, start thinking of deflecting compliments as the equivalent of rejecting a gift someone gives you. Deflecting a compliment is figuratively saying, "No, no, I don't want this kind, considerate thing you've given me. Here, take it back." Deflection is like giving the compliment-giver an unappreciative cold shoulder.

Second, write the mantra "I accept compliments with ease and grace" somewhere where you can see it daily. I used this mantra in my own life to retrain myself several years ago. For months, the mantra hung on a chalkboard next to my bathroom sink as a daily reminder to cherish the words of affirmation given to me by others.

Third, notice when you hear or see someone accept a compliment with ease and grace. Take a moment to allow their response to cement in your mind. You might even document the words they used so you can borrow them later. Observing someone who is skilled in an area where you struggle can be extremely educational and expansive. My friend Bryn is a great example. At her birthday, the attendees went around and offered Bryn admiration, and I marveled at how genuinely and softly she accepted the outpouring of kind words. Anytime you see someone modeling something you seek to be better at, take note. This is not about copying their precise style but rather being expanded into the possibility that if they can do it, you can, too.

Finally, it's time to begin practicing a simple, polite response, free of any extra verbal clutter. When someone offers you a compliment, less is more. All you need to say is "Thank you." Practice this while smiling warmly at the person who offered the compliment and making good eye contact with them. This will feel uncomfortable at first, but after you get the hang of it, accepting compliments with ease and grace will start to feel good.

If you feel compelled to say more than a simple thank you, you could also try "Thank you; that makes me feel special" and even "Thank you; I appreciate you saying that."

Practicing receiving and being with positive emotions without deflecting them creates more space for positive vibes to enter your life—and for giving genuine compliments to others. Each time you accept a compliment with ease and grace, rather than deflecting it, you are telling the Universe, "Yes, please, more of this!"

Collecting Love Nudges

One of my favorite exercises to offer anyone trying to increase their capacity for higher-vibe emotions is to recognize and track the daily love nudges in your life. Love nudges are little winks from the Universe that remind us that the energy of love is always available to us. They are overt or covert displays of love, care, and compassion. Love nudges are always happening all around you; it is your job to notice and expect them.

Here's how it works: Create a new note in your phone's note app and label it "Love Nudges" or something else that feels good to you. As you get started with this practice, be meticulous about making a note anytime someone does something big or small that demonstrates care for you.

You can start by making a note when you receive a compliment. This allows you to acknowledge the compliment and let its goodness sink in. Next, be on the lookout for tiny nudges in your everyday life. This is where the practice becomes more intricate. Increasing your awareness will require you to become acutely aware of the little love nudges that happen all the time.

For instance, if a stranger holds the door open for you at the bank, that's a love nudge; document it. If a child or a dog shows you interest, that's a love nudge; write it down.

One of my favorite love nudges was during the thick of the COVID-19 pandemic when I paid a visit to one of my favorite neighborhood coffee shops. I ordered a drip coffee with oat milk, and I watched as the barista poured in the oat milk and gave it a quick stir with a tiny wooden stick. My fellow coffee drinkers will recognize that this is not commonplace in coffee shops. Typically, your milk is carelessly poured into the drink and left to float on the top. Because I am a ninja love nudge recipient, I instantly noticed that she had gone the extra mile by stirring my drink. I not only recognized the love nudge, but I called it out. "Wow, thank you for stirring the milk. That's the extra mile," I said, then added, "I feel so loved!" The barista beamed. I could tell it was unlikely that anyone else had recognized her small gesture. My recognition and acknowledgment of her love nudge extended the good feeling for both of us.

Once you get used to this as a practice, you'll no longer need to document the tiny nudges. Recognizing these nudges will become second nature, and you'll simply smile and let it sink in. Plus, creating this little love bank serves as a database that you can refer to if you ever need a smile.

This is not to be confused with a gratitude practice, which helps you track awe and delight throughout your day. I also recommend a daily gratitude practice as a way to recognize and celebrate the small wonders in your life.

Tracking Glimmers

You've likely been introduced to the concept of a gratitude practice already. There are so many ways to implement gratitude in your life. You can start by writing three things you are grateful for in your journal each day. Any form of practicing gratitude can help contribute to your capacity to appreciate good things in your life.

I find a lot of gratitude practices can feel high level as we tend to group things we're grateful for into larger categories. Although showing gratitude en masse for your family, job, friends, pets, et cetera is important, I want to reprogram you to begin noticing the micro-gratitudes or "glimmers" that you may currently be ignoring. If you're like me, you've spent a great deal of time as a drinker blissfully unaware of your surroundings. This practice can help you tune back into your awareness. I also spent much of my time as a drinker in victim mentality. The opposite of victimhood is gratitude, and to shift your mindset you'll need to slow down and become hyperaware of the daily glimmers that bring you delight.

Begin by tracking the sensations in your body: sight, sound, touch, smell, and taste. When you see, hear, feel, smell, or taste something that brings you pleasure, take a moment and delight in the possibility that this moment was divinely created for you.

For instance, when you take your first sip of coffee in the morning, indulge in the smell and the taste. Pretend you're in a cheesy coffee commercial, and let your eyes close and allow a soft smile to fall over your face as you hold your warm, steamy mug to your mouth. Feel gratitude for this simple pleasure. Practice this throughout your day by opening your awareness to the intricate little glimmers that delight you. Notice the gorgeous flower on your morning walk. Imagine it was placed there solely for your delight, and say thank you to the Universe for this simple pleasure. When you find the perfect spot of sunshine during your walk, pause and let the light wash over you. This is literally your moment to bask in the light.

As with the love nudge exercise, looking for glimmers increases your overall capacity for good feelings. If we're always waiting for one big thing to come along to make us feel grateful, we miss the opportunities to spot all the small things that will add up over time. Each and every ounce of gratitude you can express is meaningful.

Celebrating Yourself

One way we can outwardly display our gratitude is to celebrate. I'm often surprised at how hesitant my clients are to celebrate themselves fully. Just as we avoid compliments, those who haven't grown their capacity for high-vibe emotions are experts at shrugging off wins and accomplishments. It certainly doesn't help that we—women, especially—are taught that we are most worthy of celebration when we fulfill traditional roles such as getting married or becoming a mother. There are so many other moments of celebration available to you. It is now your assignment to start recognizing and taking advantage of them.

If you are one of the many who is not used to holding space for emotions like pride, or you've coded celebrating yourself as cocky or self-absorbed, it only makes sense that you might bring alcohol into the mix to subconsciously fight off your ability to fully experience your accomplishments.

Although I'm not encouraging you to go around gloating about your life, it's important that you acknowledge your successes in a way that feels good. This habit will allow you more space to call in experiences worthy of celebration.

To begin, we need to create a space for you to be comfortable celebrating your wins alone. There are several easy ways you can accomplish this. I love the practice I created of sending myself voice memos or video messages on my phone. For example, the day I signed with my literary agent and the day I received the publishing offer for this book are two epic milestones in my life. I was so freaking proud of myself. Before I told anyone else, I wanted to capture the essence of that feeling in its most pure and raw state. So I shot quick selfie videos on my phone (for my eyes only), telling myself what just happened and how it felt. I'm in tears in the videos, and I have those little video diary entries to look at anytime I want to step back into those epic moments. I love creating these video diary entries because they capture the full range of emotion in those moments. However, if you're not keen on this idea, you could just as easily make a voice note on your phone or an old-fashioned written journal entry. I've made a practice out of doing this for all my big wins so that I can document the joy of these special moments. For smaller wins, create notes in your phone so that you can document them quickly and in the moment. If you can't tell, I want you to get super comfortable with acknowledging and celebrating the small things because this grows your capacity to receive.

In particular, I encourage you to notice and celebrate how you begin to show up differently for emotional life experiences as you embark on your alcohol-free journey. For example, my client Tiffany celebrated a moment where she brushed off a minor fender bender with grace, noting that she would have let the experience entirely derail her a mere few months earlier when she was still drinking.

Another great exercise is to find a hype squad (or person) with whom you are comfortable sharing wins. I often offer to serve as a surrogate hype squad for my clients as they build up this practice. I encourage clients to send me messages to share wins, big and small, so that we can celebrate together.

It's important that you choose your hype squad wisely. Choose people who are guaranteed to celebrate with enthusiasm. Avoid sending these wins to someone like a close friend or family member who frequently finds reasons to thwart your good news.

Increasing your capacity for and comfort with experiencing emotions at both ends of the spectrum is one of the most surefire ways to optimize your experience on this planet. The ability to show up for yourself and the intensity of your emotions is a rare act of rebellion in a world where we're frequently encouraged to numb out with alcohol, food, media, work, relationships, and any other means of distraction we might find. Your willingness to fully experience your emotions is a beautiful act of bravery and self-love. By showing self-compassion and awareness, you are laying the groundwork to experience life on an entirely new level. Your ability to show up in this way for yourself will also allow you to show up more profoundly in every other area of your life. I'm proud of you for taking this step to unbottle and embrace your emotional potential.

Becoming more emotionally intelligent and resilient can have the awesome effect of improving your relationships. You'll notice that as you become more emotionally aware, you are showing up in your relationships differently, eliciting new responses in existing relationships, and even attracting new types of relationships into your life. This will take time, and it's common to be skeptical of your ability to maintain your existing friendships and attract new ones in the early stages of sobriety. In the next chapter, I'll teach you how sobriety will help you expand into your true potential as a friend.

CHAPTER 8

Solid, Not Liquid, Bonds

Cultivating Fulfilling Friendships as a Nondrinker

Three signs of a good friend: you do not have
to perform for them; they hold space for you during
struggles; they are truly happy for your success.

Yung Pueblo

Once I overcame the fear that my social life would tank as the result of my abstinence from alcohol, I had to grapple with a very real adjacent fear: that sobriety would make me a social outcast. You already know that I'd recently moved to Austin, Texas, around the time I decided to go alcohol-free. I'd spent the first year and a half as a Texan making friends with the young, successful party crew. Although I could see some possibility in a few of the connections, there were others that I just knew were doomed for failure. I struggled to see a way to maintain friendships that were built around a boozy weekend social scene, but I also didn't want to be *that girl* who dipped out of society because she no longer drank.

By this point, I'd been studying with spiritual teachers, including Gabrielle Bernstein and Marianne Williamson, and was a fledgling student of the metaphysical text *A Course in Miracles*. Recall that the Course teaches that there is no order in the difficulty of miracles, meaning that in any situation, big or small, a miracle is available to you. I mentioned earlier that the Course says a miracle is as simple as a shift in your perception. In this sense, you can pray for a higher power to intervene, reorganizing any unhelpful or suboptimal thoughts that are no longer serving you. In many cases, asking for a miracle even opens up the space for others to change their behavior without your physical intervention.

Socially, I could see no path forward that didn't require the help of a miracle. So I prayed,

Dear Universe,

I'm feeling stuck and nervous about my friendships as I pursue this new path of sobriety. I need a miracle. Please help me see this differently. Please show me what to do and how to think about my current friendships. Show me where to direct my energy and where to release it. Thank you, Universe, for guiding me and showing me a way forward.

And so it is.

When it comes to navigating your existing friendships as an alcohol-free person, it's important that you avoid fearful assumptions and judgments (both of yourself and others). Instead, I invite you to ask for the support of the Universe, a spirit, God, angels, or whatever spiritual entity you most resonate with. If you're uncomfortable praying to a spiritual entity, I welcome you to pray to your Inner Guide.

Unsurprisingly, after my prayer for a miracle, my friendships started to shift. Two of my closest party friends randomly began joining me at the gym for a workout before dawn. To be clear, I *did not* ask them to do this; they just started showing up. What's more, the one hour I spent with those two girlfriends every week-day morning, sweating and barely talking during our group fitness class, was more nourishing and fulfilling than the innumerable hours we'd spent barhopping on the weekends. My girlfriends also began arranging weekend hikes and walks around the lake. Everywhere I turned, there were opportunities to experience my existing friendships in new ways.

Here's where the miracles got super cool: Within my friend group, there were a few specific friends I was most worried about. I perceived them to be the most set-in-their-ways, booze-loving members of my crew, and I spent a lot of time worrying about how they would react to my sudden decision to abstain. I worried I'd be the focus of gossip and judgment and instantly began making up stories about how these relationships were doomed for failure. The miracle was that even though these specific friends didn't change their drinking, they each showed up to support me in surprising ways.

One of them went out of her way to make sure there were non-alcoholic beverages on a party boat she'd rented for her birthday. Another texted to say she'd shared my Instagram handle with a woman she met who wanted to quit drinking. One of the friends I was initially worried about forwarded me articles about the alcohol-free movement. Of course, I had other buddies who were equally supportive, but how miraculous was it that the friends I'd made up fearful stories about turned out to make kind, supportive gestures?

Although I didn't remain close with all the friends from my original party crew, these little miracles were enough to help me see past my fear that all my friendships were doomed to fail. Before you jump to conclusions about your existing friendships, I encourage you to be open to the possibility that miracles are available to you and that people will often surprise you.

ALLOW FRIENDSHIPS TO TRANSFORM OR DISSOLVE

My experience is a powerful example of how you can create space to allow existing friendships to transform or dissolve. As we learned in chapter 6, it's likely that your social interests will change and evolve as a nondrinker. It's only expected that your friendship needs will evolve as well. If you're anxious about precisely how you'll allow your existing friendships to transform or dissolve, just follow my three-step method for navigating existing friendships in sobriety:

Step 1: **Take inventory.** Do an inventory of your existing friendships. In my courses, I lead an exercise that I call The Inventory™, and you can use it to help evaluate relationships of any kind. Here's how it works: Fold a sheet of paper in half to create two columns. I like to label the left column "More of This" and the right column "Less of That." (I'll call these More or Less lists moving forward.) In the More column, list the characteristics of your current friendships that you enjoy and value. In the Less column, list the characteristics of your current friendships that you struggle with.

As you do this, take some time to recognize which of your existing friendships you find most energizing and fulfilling and which are most draining.

Step 2: **Take the initiative.** Make a note of a few of the friendships you identified as most energizing and fulfilling in step 1 of this process. Now it's time to take the initiative in making these friendships stronger. Because you are the one initiating positive change in your life, you must be willing to take responsibility for the growth of your relationships as well. As you learned in my earlier example, you have the power to ask for spiritual intervention in the form of a miracle. This step can drastically transform your existing relationships with little physical intervention on your behalf.

However, to make sure you're properly nurturing your relationships, I encourage you to take the initiative by also intentionally investing in these specific relationships. Be proactive and set aside time in your schedule for friend dates. In the beginning stages, I encourage you to get comfortable managing the terms of your hangouts. This can be accomplished by focusing your friend dates on activities where neither of you will drink, such as grabbing a coffee or going for a walk. As you gain confidence, extend these dates to include activities like brunch or dinner, as long as you are prepared for and comfortable with them ordering a drink. If you want to change the ways in which you connect with someone, you're responsible for initiating the change. If you'd prefer doing activities where you're both alcohol-free, tell them! You are responsible for creating and communicating new boundaries. In being intentional about your hangouts, you'll notice yourself becoming more present as a friend.

Step 3: **Take a step back.** If you had relationships that were centered around drinking, they will inevitably experience some growing pains as you explore living an alcohol-free lifestyle. However, this doesn't mean they are doomed to failure. When it comes to the friendships you identified as more difficult, it's okay to take a step back and invest less of your time and energy in these relationships as you find your footing as an alcohol-free person. There's no need to have dramatic conversations with these friends. Instead, take some space to breathe and reassess what kind of connection—if any—with these people will feel good moving forward.

You might have an experience like mine, where the friendships you had little faith in end up transforming in surprising ways. Or you might find that these friendships fade away organically. However, I encourage you to use your best judgment, considering the depth and closeness of the friendships. I'm certainly not suggesting you ghost or avoid someone with whom you had a close relationship. It's important that you keep your integrity and communicate with others as lovingly as possible if you need space, particularly if they are reaching out to connect.

You can use the prayer I shared earlier in this chapter for guidance on your relationships. You can also do a simple cord-cutting visualization to help you metaphysically sever the cord that binds you to another. This is particularly helpful for relationships where you fear there might be some conflict. *You can find a custom cord-cutting meditation on the resources webpage for this book: amandakuda.com/unbottledresources.*

It's normal to feel intimidated about what your relationships might look like without alcohol in the picture. It's easy to jump to the worst-case scenario and worry that your relationships won't survive without drinking involved. If this is the case, the bitter truth is that your relationships were not that strong to begin with. If your friends are going to judge or abandon you for choosing to be alcohol-free, point blank: you deserve better friends. When it comes to relationships, I can promise you one thing with confidence: **No sustainable relationship is built upon a liquid bond. If you think alcohol is the glue that holds any relationship together, think again.**

Alcohol blocks true connection, healing, and vulnerability in existing relationships by creating an invisible barrier that keeps relationships from reaching true depth and achieving growth. Even in relationships where you feel closeness, you inevitably leave potential on the table if alcohol is involved.

YOUR VIBE ATTRACTS YOUR TRIBE

You may have found it difficult to consider changing your relationship with alcohol because it feels like everyone in the world drinks just the same as you. The reality is everyone in your *cur-*

rent social circle probably does drink just the same as you. That's because like attracts like, or as the old spiritual saying goes: "Your vibe attracts your tribe."

In this sense, you have unintentionally magnetized a group of like-minded, like-behaving friends who vibrate at a similar energetic frequency. You have likely surrounded yourself with a group of people with similar behaviors and values based on your stage of life and geographic location.

When stuck at a specific frequency, you also operate with skewed perception, calibrated to observe more of what is familiar. Therefore, it might *appear* that it will be impossible to find friends or lovers whose pastimes do not center around drinking. This is not true; it is only your current tunnel vision. New, like-minded, higher-vibe friends are orbiting around you at this very minute. You are currently unable to see these individuals because they are outside of your perception.

The good news is that once you have shifted your focus to improving your energetic vibration, you'll begin attracting individuals ready to match your new energetic frequency. Once you've realigned to a new energy, the Universe will get to work matching you to new, like-energy friends.

Just as you will become a magnet for individuals vibrating at similar energies, you'll also start to repel those who aren't. It's for this precise reason that some of your existing friendships may peacefully and organically fade away.

FRIENDSHIPS INFLUENCE YOUR POTENTIAL

You've probably heard Jim Rhon's philosophy that "you are the average of the five people you spend the most time with." In this sense, the people you surround yourself with have the capacity to either lift you up or keep you tethered to your comfort zone. Subconsciously, we tend to calibrate our potential to what is consistent with our current surroundings. Therefore, if you've surrounded yourself with individuals who are complacent or stuck in various situations, you might be influenced to play small. We do this out of an ancient quest for acceptance and self-preservation. Basically, we assume that we'll be rejected from the tribe or make others feel bad if we step too far outside the unspoken level of success permissible in our current social group.

If you aspire to grow and rise, it's important that you integrate yourself into social groups where higher levels of success are encouraged and expected. As you pursue your potential, this means you will be best served if you consciously surround yourself with like-minded individuals who are on a similar path. If you don't have these connections in your network already, it's imperative that you begin to take action to call them in. Connecting with other individuals in various stages of pursuing their potential will help you see what's possible, stay inspired, and keep momentum on your personal growth journey.

CALL IN NEW FRIENDSHIPS

After I made a long-term commitment to being alcohol-free, I knew that I wanted to call some new, aligned friendships into my world. I didn't mind if these new friends drank alcohol; I just didn't want drinking to be the central hub of our friendship. In addition, because I was on a spiritual and personal development path, I had begun to desire friends who shared similar interests.

Since my prayer to the Universe had been so successful before, I decided to call on this method again. I said,

Dear Universe,

Thank you for guiding me toward new, high-vibe, supportive friendships. Thank you for opening my eyes to opportunities to connect with like-minded people who will support my growth and encourage my success. Please direct my attention to the

places I should go and the people I should meet. I am open
to receiving your guidance and direction.

And so it is.

Before I knew it, new friendship opportunities were being presented to me left and right. My current friends introduced me to connections who were also interested in health and wellness. I connected with fun, high-vibe women at the dog park, juice bar, coffee shop, and nail salon. New friendship opportunities were all around; I just hadn't been fully open and available to them before.

Today, I have a crew of inspiring, supportive, high-vibe friends I love and adore. Through these friendships, I've grown and expanded in ways I'd never thought possible. I've also become more vulnerable and considerate as a friend. If you're ready to uplevel your friendships and call in a new, like-minded network that will help you grow into your potential, try implementing this four-step method for calling in new friendships in sobriety:

Step 1: **Update your inventory.** If you look back to The Inventory™ exercise you completed in reference to your existing friendships, it's probable that some of the characteristics you'd like to see in your friendships moving forward are not on the list. Add them now. For instance, if you're like me and are hoping to find friends who share your interest in spirituality or some other topic, add this to the list. Return frequently to add new desired characteristics. For example, when I left my corporate job a few years ago to start my coaching business, I made it a priority to attract more entrepreneurial friends, so I added that to the list. Over the past few years, I've also had a desire to explore femininity and sensuality more closely, so I added these characteristics to my friendship inventory in an effort to call in friends who also embody and value these concepts.

Miraculously, the Universe continues to deliver, serendipitously connecting me with new friendships that meet my evolving desires.

Step 2: **See your own light.** You can only attract what you believe you are worthy of. For the longest time, I didn't consider myself a very good friend. If I'm being honest, Party Girl Amanda was incapable of being the type of friend I am today. I was selfish and easily distracted and more concerned with the constant drama I seemed to have going on in my life than with supporting my friends. Although I had a broad friend network, many of my friendships were surface level because I was subconsciously performing to seem cool.

When it came time to attract new friendships, I knew that an important step was to see myself differently. One great way to do this is to revisit the More list from The Inventory™ and recognize that the light you see in others is merely a reflection of the light that exists in you. In other words, the reason you see and value the positive characteristics you listed is that you also have those traits in you. No matter what you have believed before, hold in your heart that you have all the makings of what you would define as a great friend. Affirm that you are deserving of fulfilling friendships that contain these characteristics, too. Make a footnote to cultivate those characteristics more intentionally in your day-to-day life.

One way you might do this is to use your list to create affirmations for yourself. Here are some examples of characteristics that might be on your More list and affirmations to go along with them:

Kind: I am kind and deserving of friends who show kindness.

Thoughtful: I am thoughtful, and I attract thoughtful friends with ease.

Generous: I am generous and surrounded by generous friends.

Declaring and affirming what you desire is a quick way to communicate your desires out into the Universe and to begin the process of calling congruent relationships in.

Step 3: **Heal your shadow.** We are all imperfect beings who constantly have opportunities to learn and grow. As you endeavor to attract stronger friendships into your life, you must also commit to doing the work that will make you a stronger friend.

One easy, if not humbling, way to get at this is to—you guessed it—review the characteristics on your Less list. Often, the characteristics that most trigger us in others—superficiality, dishonesty, unreliability—are repressed or disowned parts of our shadow self. Therefore, relationships that trigger us are brought into our lives to help us recognize opportunities for healing and growth. If you notice you've attracted multiple friendships that have similar perceived negative characteristics, this is an opportunity to get to work.

Look at each negative characteristic you've listed and ask, How might this be a piece of my own personality I've disowned or repressed? It's important that you get clear on why certain characteristics trigger you so you can learn from them and heal. Close relationships are always our mirror for learning more about ourselves. When a friend holds up a mirror to our shadow, it's easy to look away and make them the villain who has done something wrong. The more enlightened thing to do is ask, Why have I attracted someone with this characteristic into my life? What are they here to teach me? How can I use this trigger as an opportunity for healing?

Your expression of these characteristics might range from subtle to overt. They might include behaviors you hold unresolved shame about or perhaps behaviors you struggle to embrace. Whatever the case, your relationships are holding up a mirror for your healing and growth in these areas. They are open opportunities for you to become more conscious and intentional in your own behaviors.

You might even find that your relationship with alcohol frequently brought out these less-savory characteristics or allowed you to ignore them.

If you feel clear that a specific characteristic on your list is not a personality trait you embody, ask how early attachment figures, such as parents or teachers, may have displayed these characteristics. Look at the characteristics that seem unfamiliar to you and ask, How might this be an area where I hold resentment toward someone in my past who has shown this same characteristic?

Ironically, while these characteristics might reflect painful relationships in your past, they also hold a sense of familiarity. Familiarity with a feeling, even when it's negative, can draw us to people. The comfort of the pain we recognize is better than the possibility of pain or bliss that is foreign. So, even though it's unintentional, it's possible you've been attracting relationships that remind you of the discomfort you already know.

For example, I have a close friend who would often call and launch into a conversation about something distressing that was going on in her life. This was frustrating because I was able to recognize that these conversations directly reminded me of an upsetting and recurring pattern in my mother. Once I realized what was distressing me about this pattern, I was able to lovingly share this with my friend, which instantly created the space for us to show up differently and strengthen our friendship.

Unsurprisingly, having a safe space to practice this conversation with a friend gave me the courage to have a similar talk with my mom from a warm, loving place.

Often, you'll find that you've attracted friends with a certain challenging characteristic into your life several times over. This is always a sign that you need to examine and heal. My teacher Gabby Bernstein says, "Show up for what's up, or it will keep coming up," meaning if you don't address your wounds and triggers, the Universe will continue to present them to you in different forms until you realize it's time to learn the lesson.

Bringing your attention to these shadow characteristics with the intention of healing them is often enough to help you begin to show up differently in your relationships. Often, all we need to shift a pattern is to become aware of it. However, it can also be valuable to seek the support of a coach or therapist when exploring more deep-rooted or nuanced shadow characteristics. Having someone on your side who is well-versed in personal healing and transformation is an incredible tool for accelerated growth.

Admittedly, this part of the exercise is not for the faint of heart, but it is incredibly important. You see, as you come to recognize both your light and your darkness, it can become easier to focus on cultivating positive characteristics and healing negative ones.

Step 4: **Belong yourself.** My dear friend and mentor Annie Lalla introduced me to the concept of "belonging yourself." Essentially, belonging yourself is taking accountability to put yourself out there so that you can meet your people. Although your people will be magnetized to you as you begin to shift your energetic vibration, you'll have a hell of a lot easier time attracting them if you begin to put effort into hanging out in spaces your prospective friends and lovers might also frequent.

Ask yourself, Where do the types of people who embody the lifestyle I desire hang out? A great place to begin will be places where people level up their physical, intellectual, and mental well-being. Check out gym classes, yoga studios, and meditation lounges. Keep your eye out for events at cultural centers and local bookstores. Download the Meetup app, or search for growth-conscious events in your area. I've had a great deal of success following hashtags and wellness influencers in my area on Instagram.

The process of belonging yourself might mean pushing through the discomfort of going to places you've not been before or striking up conversations with strangers. Remember, as you partake in this process, that growth on this level often feels uncomfortable because it requires you to shed old ways of being and stretch into new practices that might not feel like a cozy fit quite yet. Trust me; it will get easier.

Expect that new people will be drawn to your new, higher-vibe energy. Expect potential new friends to approach you. However, this doesn't let you off the hook for doing the work yourself. Make a practice of introducing yourself to someone you feel drawn to in each new space you enter. You can start by asking a simple question about the particular space you're in. One of my go-to conversation starters is a variation of the classic pickup line, "Do you come here often?" It might be a line right out of a pickup artist's playbook, but that's because it works. I'll often find someone in a room who feels warm and interesting and ask if they've been to this event or yoga class or place before and probe them on what to expect.

As you're meeting new people, it is your responsibility to make the close. If you enjoyed a conversation with someone, tell them and ask for their phone number or Instagram (or other social media) handle. Ask if they'd be interested in getting together soon, and take it upon yourself to follow up and make plans. They will be flattered! It's rare that people make this effort, especially in adult life.

Where to Meet Like-Minded Friends

I've cultivated friendships with many people who are nondrinkers, but I don't find sobriety to be an essential connection point for my friendships, although I no longer hang out with many people who drink heavily. Transitioning to friendships with more mindful individuals did require me to seek out new people in new places. A great place to start is to visit places where growth-focused individuals hang out in your area.

Expect to put in a little work here. Start to follow hashtags on Instagram, such as #SoberInAustin (of course switching out the name of your city). I've met most of my alcohol-free friends via Instagram. Many are in my local area, but I also have a slew of alcohol-free friends all over the world due to my connections on Instagram. *I'll keep an updated list of my favorite Instagram accounts for creating community on the resources webpage for this book: amandakuda.com/unbottledresources.*

Here are some other creative places to look for new friends:

- Keep an eye on on apps like Meetup and Eventbrite to stay in the know about opportunities in your area.

- Check out the bulletin board at your favorite coffee shop or juice shop or health food store.

- Sign up for event notifications at your local bookstore, and keep an eye out for nonfiction authors to roll through your town on tour.

- Join Facebook Groups for your favorite podcasters and authors. Introduce yourself and see if any fellow fans are in your area.

- Look for hobby-focused classes in your area. This is a great way to fill your time, tap back into your creativity, and meet others with similar interests.

CULTIVATE CONNECTION

You are deserving of fulfilling relationships rooted in reciprocity and growth. Your relationships, be they with family, friends, or lovers, are meant to reflect your truest potential. Your relationships are here to support you and expand you into the most authentic, expressed version of yourself. Relationships like these celebrate your quirks and oddities and hold a nonjudgmental space for areas where you have room to grow.

In relationships such as these, you should not have to perform or dilute yourself to be accepted, appreciated, or liked. In these types of relationships, you will not need to question your worth or take a stand for your value. Although relationships of this caliber will indeed take work, the work will bring you pride and fulfillment. You will feel supported, loved, seen, and appreciated. These are the types of friendships that will create space for you to expand into your potential.

Just a few years ago, I would have looked at the above paragraphs and rolled my eyes. I would have made a mental laundry list of all the reasons relationships like this were not available to me. Today, I am proud to say that I have cultivated relationships that do indeed live up to this vision. As I look around at my friendships, I feel unbelievably connected and fulfilled. I have a network of friends who are incredibly supportive. They cheer for me as I strive for my dreams and hold me when I am struggling with grief, confusion, or pain of any kind.

As a drinker, I was not available for the caliber of relationships I have attracted into my life today. I was caught up in popularity and social status versus connection. I was unclear on my relationship values, so I unwittingly stuck around for friends who were not a match for my needs. I was terrible at boundaries and, frankly, not great at reciprocity in most of my friendships. I was counting on high-status friendships to make me feel worthy, conveniently ignoring my ability to cultivate self-worth and love within myself.

As you embark into new places, remember the Universe is already at work with its friendship matchmaking skills, but it is your job to belong yourself, be bold, and start conversations. Rest assured: your people are out there. Going alcohol-free is a call for more intentional, solid bonds. After a lifetime of feeling like a social outcast who was constantly performing to fit in, I finally feel like I am surrounded by friendships where I am celebrated for showing up as my authentic self. I have never felt more connected and supported in my relationships than I do as an alcohol-free woman. My friends have served as catalysts for my growth and have each been true champions of my potential. You deserve friendships like these. You can only rise to the potential you see possible around you; therefore, it is essential that you make a practice of improving your existing relationships and calling in new, like-minded friendships as well.

The way you show up in your friendships creates the groundwork for how you'll show up in your romantic relationships. In the next chapter, I'll teach you how to expand on these principles to cultivate lasting, fulfilling romantic relationships.

CHAPTER 9

Love without the Hangover

Navigating Sober Dating, Partnerships, and Sex

We need connection, but first we need
to connect with ourselves.

Holly Whitaker, *Quit Like a Woman*

Romantic relationships are one of life's greatest containers for personal growth because—like friendships—they serve as a divine mirror for both our shadow and our light. However, a romantic partnership reflects where we might grow and expand in a magnified way that other relationships cannot. Your romantic partnerships are intended to be a container that supports your growth, healing, and self-expression.

Yet if you have been relying on alcohol as a mechanism for romantic connection, there is no doubt that you have yet to access the depth of vulnerability and growth available to you in your current or past romantic relationships. If so, it may feel intimidating to approach your love life without the support of a cocktail or glass of wine. Stick with me; I want to share with you how exploring romantic relationships can wholeheartedly improve your romantic life in ways you never deemed possible.

If you're like me, you've come to equate drinking with sexiness, sophistication, romance, and seduction. I had absolutely no idea what my romantic life would look like without alcohol, but I can assure you that I wasn't overly optimistic. My lack of optimism lay chiefly in my judgment toward people who didn't drink. If you had asked me to date a nondrinker during my Party Girl days, I would have scoffed at the idea, assuming the person was either boring as hell or someone I'd have to watch my drinking around to avoid triggering them (which, to be clear, I was not interested in). With an attitude like that, it's no wonder I projected my past judgments onto others and created negative stories about what potential romantic partners might think of me as a nondrinker.

Regardless of your current relationship status, I know that you, too, are likely uncertain about what might happen to your romantic life when you give up alcohol. Perhaps you worry that your past judgments about nondrinkers will be projected onto you. Maybe you're worried about managing your nerves or feeling comfortable around a romantic partner. You might even be completely unsure how you'll muster up the courage to be flirtatious or seduce your partner without the little added help you've been getting from alcohol.

Let me assure you, when it comes to dating and relationships, I've heard it all (and lived a lot of it, too). In this chapter, I'll address the biggest fears I hear from both single and partnered individuals who want to explore the world of elective sobriety. I'll offer you subtle mindset shifts and tools to address your current fears and allow you to step more fully into your romantic potential.

DATING WITHOUT LIQUID COURAGE

Remember when I told you that I was gawky and taller than all the boys in high school? Well, I'm not exaggerating when I say that I never got asked on a single date until well after I was in college and out of my awkward ugly duckling stage.

Because I began drinking in my late teens, every single one of my formative romantic experiences was fueled by alcohol. Every first date, first kiss, first sexual encounter was sponsored by liquid courage. Therefore, I can assure you that I am highly qualified to teach you about how to date sober because I had to learn the process from scratch as a thirty-year-old woman. So it is with much research, along with humbling trial and error, that I bring to you hope that dating is not only possible without alcohol but also quite magnificent.

Benefits of Dating Alcohol-Free

Dating alcohol-free will inevitably open you up to a new world of learning and growth opportunities. You will be confronted with discomforts that you didn't know existed, and you'll also need to create new frames through which to view your dating experiences. In this section, I'll guide you through the mindset and behavior changes that will help you create a kick-ass, alcohol-free dating life that you're proud of.

You act more authentically. As I reflect on my days as a Party Girl, I was emotionally unavailable and not quite ready to be an outstanding partner. I was desperately afraid of vulnerability and judgment, so I played out the role I thought my partner wanted in most of my relationships.

None of my early romantic partners were getting the real me because I wasn't even certain who that was. But your romantic partners deserve the most authentic version of you. The right romantic partner will see the inherent beauty in your vulnerability and perfect imperfection. They will be delighted by the quirks and awkwardness you are trying to dim through drinking.

Without question, I have become a stronger romantic partner as a nondrinker. Being alcohol-free has created the space for me to work through my unrealized attachment wounds and suboptimal ways of showing up in a relationship. Sobriety has forced me to tune in to my authentic desires and show up more vulnerably. I know that the version of me any potential partner meets today is inevitably a better match than the person I was as a Party Girl. So, even though I still struggle with confidence and find myself being triggered or confused, I can say with absolute certainty that the alcohol-free version of me is a great catch. Why? Because, for better or worse, my potential partners are getting the true me. Most importantly, they're getting a version of me who is conscious and willing to show up and put in the work. I also know that I am unquestionably a better date and that I cultivate better dating experiences as a nondrinker.

When I honestly assess who I was as a romantic partner while drinking, I wasn't the best version of myself. I was impulsive, emotional, insecure, immature, and dramatic. Although I thought drinking made me more fun and carefree, it also exacerbated my lesser qualities, none of which made me an attractive romantic partner.

Sobriety is sexy. If you're like me, you've probably worried about what potential romantic partners will think about your decision to abstain from alcohol. You've even wondered if potential romantic partners will judge you or if sobriety will make you undatable. Worry not; while sobriety is your superpower in all areas of life, it is particularly so when it comes to dating.

I remember one of my first serious love interests as a sober woman back in the fall of 2017, my first year as a nondrinker. He and I met on a dating app, and although I was still figuring out the sober dating thing, I disclosed to him early on that I was spending the entire year alcohol-free. I'll never forget the look in his eyes when I explained my decision to abstain from alcohol and how much I was learning in the process. His mouth formed a half smile, and I knew in that moment he thought my decision to be alcohol-free was sexy as hell. He even said as much and was one of my biggest supporters when it came to my sharing about my alcohol-free journey online. Even though our relationship wasn't a long-term fit, I am so grateful to him for creating a space where I could feel confident and sexy in my new lifestyle.

This experience wasn't an anomaly. In my relationships as a sober woman, my partners have all seen my alcohol-free lifestyle as a value-add. In fact, I choose to believe my decision to abstain makes me a magical unicorn who stands out from the crowd. I can recount multiple times when dates have shared their admiration of my commitment to living an alcohol-free life. For the men I date who are good matches, my sobriety is sexy.

You feel the feels. You've probably been taught that liquid courage is an acceptable and necessary way to get through nerve-racking first dates. I like to look at it another way: I believe nervousness is your friend when it comes to your love life. As you learned in chapter 7, all emotions have intelligence, and it's particularly important to get comfortable with the emotional signals your body is sending you when you're searching for a life partner.

In this sense, anxiety, nervousness, and every other emotion that comes up in romantic encounters are there to offer you guidance. After all, how are you supposed to know how you feel about someone if you've numbed your ability to feel?

How often have you continued a relationship with someone longer than you should have because you weren't clear whether they were a match or not? For that matter, how many times have you slept with someone you otherwise would not have been attracted to because you were under the influence of alcohol? Approaching dating scenarios with a clear head is the most reliable way to avoid either of these situations. Further, if the date is not enjoyable, having a sober mind will empower you to exit the date as early as possible, versus dragging the experience on because you're slightly numb.

My client Nina is a great example of someone who has benefitted from feeling her feelings when dating. When we started working together, it was clear to me that Nina was investing a lot of time in trying to figure out if the guys she was dating liked her and obsessing over what she could do to earn their interest. The problem was that Nina was so disconnected from her own feelings that she could not discern if *she* liked *them*. With alcohol out of the way, I was able to lead her through The Inventory™ and help her tap into her feelings so that she could understand if she was actually interested in the men she was dating or if she was just choosing romantic partners because *they* were interested in her.

You attract stronger partnerships. Most of my relationships during my drinking days had repeat themes and were overall unfulfilling partnerships that I was trying to make work because I feared I'd end up alone. When it came down to it, I settled for substandard behavior in my romantic partners because I settled for substandard behavior in myself. Time after time, I attracted emotionally unavailable Peter Pan types who weren't ready to be the partner I needed.

When I first stepped back onto the dating scene as a sober woman, I was completely unclear about what I wanted in a partner. Therefore, I didn't limit my dating pool at all, opening myself right back up to the same Peter Pan types I'd spent the past decade chasing after.

I initially thought I'd position myself as the "cool chick" who was fine with dating anyone. I learned quickly that this was an idealistic approach and a notable learning opportunity. I realized that I was no longer attracted to the same type of partner I had been drawn to as a drinker. The magnanimous party boy who spent his weekends out on the town was clearly no longer for me.

Likewise, men who drank more than moderately were not a good fit. I swiftly eliminated men who glamorized drinking or identified it as a hobby or important pastime. I still date men who drink, just not men who make drinking a priority. I encourage you to be discerning about the personality traits and characteristics you value in a romantic partner at this stage of your life. You are upleveling your life, and you deserve to spend time with romantic partners who are at least interested in doing the same.

I recommend you complete The Inventory™ exercise I shared in chapter 8 to get clear on what you desire in your romantic relationships. Completing this exercise will make it easier to recognize your person when you meet them. Likewise, it will serve as a concrete reminder of what types of partners you are no longer interested in as well as identify patterns and personal growth opportunities.

It's important to note that as you upgrade your expectations, you will inevitably have a more select pool of potential matches to choose from. This is a good thing, although you might find it discouraging at first. As you enter the dating scene, make this your mantra: "Amazing potential romantic partners are around me everywhere." From this perspective, you'll open your eyes to new opportunities to connect with individuals everywhere you go.

You truly connect. Many of us have fallen victim to the lie that we won't even be able to meet our person if we don't conform to the socially acceptable dating standard of "meeting for drinks." We're taught that liquid courage is the antidote for surviving first dates, and we've been brainwashed to believe that booze is a necessary aphrodisiac for romantic encounters. This is untrue. In fact, after going on my share of sober dates, I'm absolutely clear that drinking gets in the way of true connection and discernment during the dating process. Although this will require some vulnerability and practice, you'll grow more confident and comfortable each time you conquer a sober date.

As you're starting to see, there are many benefits to being sober and single. Now it's time to get out there and start dating so that you can reap the reward. Even though I was apprehensive at first, I can honestly say that I love sober dating. However, it's taken me a while to ditch some of the old, tired dating paradigms I upheld as a drinker and figure out a better way. I spent the early months of my sober dating days making every faux pas in the book. From whom I chose to date to how I attempted to disclose my alcohol-free lifestyle to the types of dates I accepted, I did all the hard work of making the mistakes for you, and I'm happy to share what worked and what didn't. The great news is, there are no mistakes when it comes to dating, but rather potential learning opportunities.

If you're entering the dating world alcohol-free for the first time, you'll probably need to slightly reframe your mindset around dating because what you were willing to tolerate as a drinker is quite likely much less than you deserve.

Guidelines for Kick-Ass Sober Dates

Talk about your lifestyle. My very first date as a sober woman was definitely one to remember. I already knew the date was doomed when he suggested we meet at a bar for happy hour without bothering to ask where I lived or worked to see if the location was convenient for me. Spoiler, the bar he chose was within walking distance from his house. I'm more of a "meet in the middle" kind of gal, but I can understand the practicality of choosing a location that's convenient and familiar, so I was willing to let it slide. Upon arriving at the agreed-upon spot, my date greeted me and invited me to order whatever I wanted on his tab.

At this early stage, I assumed it was best to be covert about my abstinence, so I casually ordered a sparkling water. When

I returned to the table, he glanced at the bottle before looking up at me and saying, "What, you don't drink? Are you like, super Christian or something?" To this day, the biggest regret of my dating life is that I wasn't quick-witted enough to slip into an exaggerated southern drawl, place my hand upon his, and say, "Yes, and I have come here today to share the Word of our Lord and Savior, Jesus Christ, with you." It would have been priceless.

Instead, I composed myself, explained to my date that I was currently abstaining and why, and did my best to assure him that I was a fun and normal gal. We proceeded to have a somewhat decent date, but you shouldn't be surprised to find that we never spoke again. It's safe to say that I could have avoided this entire encounter had I just been open and up front about my lifestyle. I would have learned that drinking was important to him and might have opted out of the date entirely.

I know you're wondering how and when to share about sobriety with potential partners; let me skip past everything I did wrong and share what I landed on. Because I am not in recovery, I do not prescribe to the philosophy that my sobriety is my number-one priority. For this reason, I choose not to lead with sobriety as my defining characteristic. On dating apps, I do not list it in my profile. In person, I do not disclose my nondrinker status in a basic introduction unless it makes sense. I also do not hide my decision to be alcohol-free. It's something I've grown to be very proud of, in fact. I simply wait for the appropriate point in a conversation to announce my lifestyle choice rather than just blurting it out.

In the best-case scenario, I find an opening when discussing interests and hobbies. In a worst-case scenario, I wait until we're deciding where to meet for a date. Either way, my go-to statement is, "I actually don't drink anymore, but I don't mind if you do as long as it's not a huge part of your lifestyle." Whatever you do, don't do what I did and hide or conveniently forget to mention your abstinence from alcohol. You'll save yourself a lot of time and awkward conversation if you just share about your alcohol-free lifestyle up front.

Don't "meet for drinks." Early on in my sober dating journey, I was overly flexible about the types of dating experiences I was open to. This often put me in dating situations that ultimately weren't conducive to connecting with a potential partner.

Even though I figured out that I needed to disclose early on that I wasn't drinking, I still agreed to several first dates where my date would have a few drinks as we got to know each other. Frequently, I found these situations to be unfulfilling. Sometimes they ended up being completely annoying. After one too many experiences in which my date imbibed a bit excessively, I decided I was over meeting for drinks. If I could be sober and slightly uncomfortable and awkward, so could my date.

With that, I made the executive decision that I was no longer meeting at places where drinks were served. Today, my go-to first date is either meeting for coffee or going on a walk. This strategy has resulted in a much more productive, relaxed, and connection-focused dating experience than meeting for drinks ever did.

To begin, coffee shops and walks are much more conducive to conversation. It's difficult to get to know someone at a crowded, noisy bar or restaurant. The casual nature of coffee shops and walking trails also releases some of the pressure you might feel in a more formal environment. Walks are my favorite way to connect because movement is relaxing and gives you an outlet for any nervous energy. Finally, meeting for coffee or a walk automatically sets your date up to stay sober without you having to ask if they'd be comfortable not drinking. Although I want you to become comfortable making this request, setting up dates where drinking isn't an option is a great workaround early on.

Here are a couple of scripts you can use if your date recommends meeting for drinks:

"I [actually don't drink anymore/am not drinking right now], but I'd love to meet up for a walk. Would that be okay?"

or

"I'm excited to meet up and get to know you better. I'm not drinking right now, and I don't mind if you do, but would you be open to a date where drinking isn't involved? I'd love to meet for coffee."

If you're going to decline meeting for drinks (which I encourage you to do), it's your responsibility to make an alternative suggestion. In a world where meeting for drinks is the norm, it's unfair to expect the average person, who has little familiarity with this new lifestyle, to be able to think on their feet and offer an alternative solution. Come prepared with a couple of coffee shops or walk locations to recommend. I also want to be clear that I don't expect my romantic partners to never drink around me; this is just an optimization tactic I use for the first few dates when we're really getting to know each other.

Use dating apps for practice. Although I think dating apps are a fine place to meet your person, I especially love apps because they offer endless opportunities to practice. One of the best ways to grow your confidence as a newly sober single person is to go on dates. There is no better way to rack up a few dates quickly than swiping on apps. Dating apps offer an endless pool of potential partners to practice with.

As you reenter the dating world sober, I encourage you to look at each dating experience as practice for The One. This way, it doesn't matter what the outcome of your date is as long as you're getting in valuable practice time. Viewing dating apps in this way is a great way to take the pressure off and give yourself some grace as you gain footing as a sober dater. It is important that you still show up with kindness and integrity, even though you're practicing. After all, you never know which date might actually be The One.

Although I have a lot of experience under my belt and have been lucky to be mentored by some of the greatest minds in the dating and relationship coaching field, I'll be the first to admit that I've gotten it wrong more than I've gotten it right when it comes to dating. There are still romantic situations in which I feel like a lost, shy teenage girl. I've had to ask my girlfriends to hold my hand while sending a vulnerable text message. I've acted from a place of insecurity and fear. Putting yourself out there, free from any opportunity to numb, is scary and hard. It's also tremendously brave and rewarding.

I've found that approaching dating with more intentionality has paid off substantially. In the end, not drinking alcohol has made me far from undatable. While I haven't met The One at the time of writing this manuscript, I have had many delightful, enlightening, and fulfilling dating experiences with wonderful men who made great dates and short-term partners but ultimately weren't a long-term match for me. I've taken my own advice and approached each of these experiences as vital practice for The One, which has allowed me to show up to each date with integrity, energy, authenticity, and intention. I've grown my confidence as a dater and become clearer on what I am looking for long term.

It might raise your optimism to know that I've also received very positive feedback from my dates. Most share that the experience of dating a nondrinker is a breath of fresh air in comparison to the predictable, surface-level dates they typically entertain. Additionally, I've found that the men I attract from this energetic stance are more emotionally available and congruent with the type of man I envision being The One.

If you want more tips on sober dating, I have an entire course devoted to teaching you about dating more mindfully. You can find it by visiting amandakuda.com/mindfuldating.

PARTNERSHIP AND MARRIAGE, MINUS THE BUZZ

The energetics of partnership is not dissimilar from that of friendship or dating. As you read through this section, remember that all the principles from the previous section apply here, but they will be tremendously amplified because long-term romantic partnerships will reflect your most uncomfortable opportunities for growth. These uncomfortable opportunities will become magnified as you begin to view them with a sober mind. Although this might feel more complicated initially, your potential as a romantic partner will only become more illuminated as you begin to show up in your partnership on a new level.

As a coach, I have found that my clients who are in partnerships express similar, recurring fears about what would happen to their existing partnerships if they elected to go sober. On the surface, they fear that their partner will hold them back from achieving their goal of living an alcohol-free lifestyle. On a deeper level, they worry that their partnership will be compromised in some way without the presence of alcohol.

It's not unusual to buy into the story that everything will be different in your relationship if you suddenly quit drinking. Many romantic relationships place tremendous importance on drinking as a means of connection. Throughout this section, I'll address some of the most common roadblocks and romantic delusions my clients encounter in their partnerships while pursuing an alcohol-free lifestyle. I'll offer you some more realistic ways to view these fears and arm you with tools that will allow you to become a stronger romantic partner. Ultimately, relationships are a collaborative effort, but you can only control how you show up. So let's make sure you are showing up as the strongest version of yourself.

If drinking has been a significant part of your romantic relationship, it's probable that you haven't quite been reaching the levels of romantic depth, vulnerability, or connection that are available to you in your partnership. I invite you to acknowledge that your relationship won't be a magical fairy tale just because you've quit drinking. You may feel vulnerable and frustrated immediately after removing the consistent buffer alcohol has provided. You may be immediately faced with tough problems you've glossed over and avoided with drinking.

With alcohol out of the way, you'll have to face these conflicts head-on. This is bound to be disarming, but rest assured, it's not impossible. If you love and care for your partner and are otherwise fulfilled by your relationship, sobriety is your invitation to dig in and do the work.

A note on abusive relationships: **the important caveat to all of what I'm about to share is that if you have been drinking alcohol to numb the pain of emotional or physical abuse from a partner, you must seek support to help you exit the relationship as quickly and safely as possible.** The remainder of what I offer here will be under the assumption that abuse is not present.

Go First, and Be Okay Going Alone

Every client I've met would prefer that their partner quit alcohol with them. Because this is such a prevalent fantasy, it's important to address some of the common pitfalls of holding on to this idea. I often see my clients trying to manipulate their relationship with their partner or inadvertently making their partner a scapegoat as they embark on their alcohol-free journey. Let's look at the three common pitfalls I see in my clients' relationships when they are trying to quit drinking.

Pitfall 1: **Finger-pointing.** Finger-pointing occurs when you transfer the focus from your drinking to your partner's drinking. This might show up in many forms, such as giving ultimatums, shaming, or judging your partner for their relationship with alcohol. My client Deidra desperately wanted her husband to quit drinking when she did. After she gave up alcohol for an extended period, she found herself getting frustrated when her husband would drink. Rather than letting the scene play out, Deidra would criticize her husband for his behaviors and nag him to quit, too. This forced a wedge between them and seemingly caused her husband to drink more out of rebellion.

Finger-pointing is most frequently counterproductive. In the end, it is a form of personal insecurity and weakness. We judge, push, and pick at someone else's habit to avoid looking at our own or to affirm that our success is reliant on their actions. In the end, unless your partner has a harmful relationship with alcohol, I encourage you to focus on your journey alone.

Ultimately, you must release the fantasy that your partner will change with you. Focus on being an example, and make no attempt to persuade your partner or shame them into changing their habits just because you have. In many cases, you may be surprised that your example encourages positive behavior change in your partner without any action on your behalf.

If you've been actively pushing your partner (or felt tempted to do so), I recommend a simple practice of spiritual release. Your spiritual assignment here is to release judgment and obsession so that you can focus solely on your side of the street. If you're game, try a simple prayer like this nightly or whenever you feel triggered by your partner's behavior:

Dear Universe,

*I'm in need of a miracle. I am feeling judgmental about
my partner's drinking. I am obsessing over their behavior.
I am ready to release these negative emotions so I can focus on*

*my own journey. Please help me release these feelings
and see them in their innocence.*

And so it is.

In this prayer practice, you are asking for your own miraculous healing, not a change in behavior from your partner. The miracle can come in many forms. It is possible your partner *will* change their behavior without any provocation on your part. It is equally as likely that your partner will not change but that you will no longer be affected by their behavior. Do not try to control the outcome. Each option will bring you equal levels of peace.

Pitfall 2: **Bandwagoning.** In relationships, bandwagoners let the lifestyle choices of their partner dictate their own lifestyle choices. This is a form of codependence. For example, my client Lacey told me she had given up alcohol with her husband several times when he was training for a big race. Lacey knew that she and her husband had very different relationships with alcohol. Although he seemed to be able to control his drinking with ease, she struggled to moderate and knew she would be better off if she gave up alcohol altogether.

Yet every time her husband went back to drinking, so did Lacey. Each time, she'd hold on to hope that moderation would be possible, only to fall right back into the same drinking pattern she was trying to escape.

Lacey was a victim of bandwagoning. She placed the success of her sobriety on her husband also being sober. In this way, Lacey continued to stray from a lifestyle she wanted to pursue. Each time she returned to drinking, her confidence took a hit. It wasn't until Lacey finally concluded that she could and would stop drinking all on her own that things in her life began to shift.

As it turns out, Lacey's husband was actually very supportive of her sobriety; she merely had to share openly about how much she felt drinking was affecting her and ask for his support. Ultimately, this support came in the form of encouragement and accountability, *not* with her husband giving up alcohol as well.

Pitfall 3: **People-pleasing.** Like bandwagoners, people pleasers rely on the actions of their partners as a cue for when they should and should not drink. My client Sara devoted a great deal of energy to making others comfortable, especially her husband, who was a moderate to heavy drinker. Sara would manage to go several weeks without alcohol only to fall back into drinking at the suggestion of her husband.

Sometimes Sara's husband would presumptively bring her a glass of wine when he poured his own, even when he knew she was practicing sobriety. Being agreeable, Sara would typically break her promise to herself because she wanted to please her husband. As you can imagine, with each failed attempt at taking a break from drinking, Sara's self-confidence shrank and her frustration grew.

In Sara's case, her husband was triggered by her decision to quit drinking and sabotaged her plans under the guise of being considerate. I asked Sara to set a firm boundary with her husband, and when she did, she was able to take a long-term break from alcohol and begin to grow her sense of independence and self-worth.

When it comes to changing your habits, the ultimate lesson is this: your actions are the only variable you can control. Hinging your success or failure on your partner's behavior in any way is a subtle way of playing the victim.

If you have found yourself obsessing over your partner's habits rather than focusing on your own, consider what underlying emotion is causing you to do so. Remember that your Inner Critic will always try to distract you and help you find ways to play small. The Inner Critic is an expert at convincing you to avoid taking accountability by shifting the blame onto someone else.

Alcohol as the Third Wheel

In so many romantic relationships, alcohol serves as an unintentional third wheel. Drinking becomes something you do as a couple, making it all the more difficult to picture what your relationship would look like if one or both of you quit drinking.

Take my client Marra, for example. Marra is a successful executive who'd come to me after several failed attempts to moderate her relationship with alcohol. While she didn't have an addiction, she often found herself drinking more than she wanted. Under the influence, she became anxious in her romantic relationship. This would cause uncomfortable conflict with her husband. Despite the consistent results, she was hesitant to quit drinking because indulging in wine was an experience she and her husband enjoyed together. The double bind created by her desire to connect with her husband and her instinct to quit drinking was confusing and frustrating for Marra.

Like many of my clients, Marra always opened a bottle of wine with the best of intentions to enjoy one lovely glass as a means to wind down for the evening. While this strategy sometimes worked, it often didn't, and she and her husband would end up bickering over something arbitrary. The next morning, Marra would drag through her workout if she didn't skip it entirely. She'd be short-tempered with her kids and drudge through tasks at work. Yet because she was an extremely high achiever, her less-than-optimal performance was rarely noticed by others.

Marra's internal state, however, was a different story. She felt distant in her relationship with her husband and their children. She felt dissatisfied with work despite constant accolades from colleagues and superiors. She felt like a stranger in her own skin and knew in her soul that this wasn't the way things were supposed to be.

I asked Marra if she was willing to believe that her husband loved her for who she was, not what she did. Meaning his love for her was not contingent on her decision to indulge in alcohol. While she agreed, it was with hesitation. Marra herself commented on how ridiculous it was; she knew her husband loved her and that she would be a better wife and mother if she weren't always numbing out with wine and operating at half capacity while nursing a hangover.

Yet she continued to bring up the concept of the connection she and her husband had over drinking. During a coaching session, I asked Marra if she and her husband ever went out for dinner. They did, of course. I asked if she and her husband often ordered precisely the same meal. They didn't. I wondered if she had ever ordered something more health conscious, while her husband had splurged. She had.

"Interesting," I commented. "Did you experience any sense of disconnection during these meals, what with you eating different entrées and all?"

Marra laughed. "No, not at all."

"You see," I explained, "your shared experience is defined by the time spent together, not by having identical experiences. If it's about having a common experience to talk about, could you not as easily share a dessert?"

I could tell my questions challenged Marra. Of course, this was the point. We've been sold the story that drinking is some sort of sacred bonding ritual. Yet, as illustrated by Marra's many experiences, alcohol continually pulled her and her husband further apart.

If you, too, have believed your partner's love for you will somehow fade once alcohol is out of the picture, remember that no sustainable relationship is built upon a liquid bond. If your relationship is strong, I'm here to sell you on the belief that your partner loves you, not the activities you partake in. A strong partner will want you to live as your most vibrant self. A partner who fights for you to dull yourself down is fighting for their own comfort, not the success of your relationship.

You deserve a partner who is supportive of your physical, mental, and spiritual health and wellness. You deserve a partner who challenges you to explore your greatness, not a partner who persuades you to stay small for their benefit.

Playing with Variables

When you remove alcohol from the picture, be conscious of other ways you might be tempted to change your behavior, specifically if having a nightly cocktail was your way of spending time with your partner. It might be tempting to use this time for something else as a way to stay distracted from the fact that you're not having a drink. Although this may be a form of self-preservation initially, be mindful of how many variables you change in your relationship.

For example, if you cancel your nightly cocktail time just because there are no longer cocktails, you automatically forfeit a valuable opportunity to connect on a deeper level. Over time, this could create unintentional distance between you and your partner. It could be tempting to blame this distance on the absence of alcohol, but in reality, *you've* changed an additional variable by opting out of your time together.

A more helpful approach would be to share with your partner that you'd like to switch things up during your regular time together. Change the location in your house where you meet, and fix yourself a delicious mocktail or a soothing cup of tea. Use this time to connect with your partner intentionally. If this feels awkward, enlist the help of a relationship card deck filled with questions you and your partner can ask each other to provoke more intimate conversations. I really love the Create the Love Cards by Mark Groves and the Where Should We Begin? game by Esther Perel. Sobriety is an opportunity to make your relationship stronger. Although you may want to engage in some additional self-care in your early days of going alcohol-free, be sure to schedule plenty of time to stay connected with your partner.

Conscious Uncoupling

My client Naomi came to me with a troubling fear about her marriage. After years of drinking, Naomi was worried that the lack of closeness between her and her husband would become glaringly obvious if she stopped. Naomi confessed that she and her husband had been married only a short while, and she'd realized they weren't a good match early on. They'd been having problems. Alcohol was a tool she used to numb the sense of discontent and separation in their relationship. She told me that she desperately wished they hadn't spent so much time drinking during their courtship. Perhaps then she wouldn't have ended up in this predicament.

As a coach, I frequently work with individuals who use alcohol to bandage their relationships. Typically, bandaging is done completely unconsciously. We reach for a drink to soothe our ego and avoid a tough realization that perhaps our relationship isn't as strong or fulfilling as we'd like it to be.

It's quite possible that your relationship with alcohol has slowly numbed your ability to be vulnerable and connect with your partner. Without this connection, it's completely logical for you to assume your relationship has lost the spark. If this sounds familiar, give yourself space to become reacquainted with and fully present to your partner before jumping to doom-and-gloom conclusions.

Likewise, I invite you to consider that your fear is rooted in truth. Perhaps you have been using alcohol to numb a very real disconnection in your relationship. Maybe, once the hazy veil of alcohol is lifted, the strains on your relationship will be all the more visible.

In my mind, this is not a failure but a tremendous opportunity. If your relationship is not serving you or your partner, wouldn't you want to know as soon as possible? Wouldn't you want to rip off the bandage and allow the wound to heal? Isn't it in your best interest to release a relationship that is no longer serving you so that you can both move on and find the loving, fulfilling partnerships you deserve?

Take my client Becca, for example. Becca was in the midst of separating from her husband when she called me to help her quit drinking. When we discussed her relationship with her estranged husband, she had an epiphany. She realized that she'd been avoiding changing her relationship with alcohol because she knew that when she did, she'd have no excuse for her marriage crumbling. Alcohol served as both an excuse and an anesthetic. With this realization in mind, Becca and I worked on celebrating the beautiful clarity that allowed her to dissolve a union that was built on a false foundation. The decision to quit drinking was the catalyst for setting both her and her husband free from a marriage that was formed from an unstable liquid bond.

Ultimately, my wish for you is that you have a loving, fulfilling relationship that provides both you and your partner with opportunities for massive personal and spiritual growth. I hold the vision for you, my reader, to have a romantic relationship that supports you in becoming the most radiant, magnificent, self-expressed version of yourself. It is my belief that the benefits of a partnership should span beyond the union of the two partners and into the lives of those around them. My stand is for your happiness and growth. If you've found that alcohol has indeed been the glue holding your relationship together, I implore you to ask, Who is this benefiting?

My beautiful friend Tammi—a prominent voice in the sober community—has spoken out publicly about her decision to uncouple from her marriage after several years of sobriety. My favorite thing about Tammi's story is how much thought and integrity she put into her uncoupling experience as a result of her growth as a sober woman. Although any separation is bound to have a bit of conflict, I was in awe of how consciously Tammi talked about the decision to dissolve her marriage.

If you have found that your sobriety is a catalyst for your uncoupling, I invite you to welcome this experience with grace and appreciation. It would not serve you or your partner to stay stuck in a relationship that is no longer contributing to your growth. Here is a short prayer you might say to support you in this transition:

Dear Universe,

*I have come to realize that it is time to uncouple from
[state your partner's name], and I need your help. Help me
face this transition with ease, grace, and appreciation.
Help me see [name] in their innocence and leave this
relationship with a new appreciation for all it has taught me.*

And so it is.

SOBER SEX

When it comes to romantic relationships, sex and physical intimacy can often feel more intimidating and inaccessible than emotional intimacy. Unless you were lucky enough to grow up in a sex-positive household where sex and sexual expression were discussed openly, you might be completely underinformed or misinformed about the world of sex and intimacy. Therefore, it makes sense that you may have believed the lie that alcohol in some way enhances your sex life.

Let's start with my armchair-expert sex ed talk. Again, I'll restate the basics: Alcohol is a depressant. This means it slows the function of your nervous system. Your sex organs are part of said nervous system. Essentially, alcohol negatively impacts the function of all your pleasure centers. Although alcohol may lower your inhibitions and blind you to your insecurities, it otherwise inhibits the sexual performance and experience of pleasure for both partners.

No matter what you've come to believe, alcohol in no way physically enhances the sensations of a sexual experience. If you're someone who feels shy or self-conscious about getting intimate without a little liquid aphrodisiac to set the mood, try following these easy steps for more confident, fulfilling sober sex:

Step 1: **Become a student of sex and sexuality.** Let's face it, the education you received about sex was probably quite dismal. If you've been faking your confidence in sexual encounters, the first step in growing your confidence is to educate yourself. Consider starting with books on sex and sexuality to better learn how the body works and inspire you to awaken your inner sexual prowess. I recommend Emily Nagoski's *Come as You Are* and Regena Thomashauer's *Pussy: A Reclamation* as great places to start. Might I also recommend that you consider consuming these books as audiobooks? I find it can help with overcoming any bashfulness you might have around certain words.

Step 2: **Practice.** If you've been using alcohol to cheat the system of intimacy and pleasure, it's probably because you're not clear on what you enjoy. Begin this practice solo with self-pleasure. Invest time exploring your own body and gaining a better understanding of what you enjoy.

Step 3: **Call out your vulnerability.** If you've used alcohol as an aphrodisiac and are nervous about sober sexual encounters, being honest with your partner is a great first step to growing your confidence. Start with something simple like "I'm feeling a little anxious and vulnerable about intimacy now that I'm not drinking, and I wanted to let you know." Then, if something specific would make you feel more comfortable, be sure to share it with your partner. Perhaps you'd like extra reassurance or for them to take the lead while you get back into your comfort zone.

Step 4: **Get curious.** As you invest time and energy into learning about sex and sexuality, you'll encounter new philosophies and ways of being that feel foreign, edgy, or entirely uncomfortable. Use your new knowledge as an opportunity to get curious about the possibilities you perhaps shut yourself off from as a result of numbing with alcohol. My good friend and sober expert Tawny Lara shares openly about her experience with exploring her sexuality and expressing herself sexually as a sober person. Sobriety opened her up to forms of sexual desire and expression that she had rejected as a drinker but finally felt brave enough to claim as she tapped into her desires in sobriety.

Step 5: **Invest in modern sex ed.** I'm so lucky to know many talented and generous sex educators who have helped reshape my understanding of what intimacy can look like and helped me become more comfortable talking about sex, sensuality, and pleasure more openly. There are extremely safe and professional environments where you can get properly caught up to speed, ask questions, and access helpful resources. You can find a host of self-guided online courses, live programs, in-person events, and excellent coaches to help reintroduce you to sexual exploration. While it might feel intimidating or edgy to invest in this type of education, sexual confidence and fulfillment are fabulous ways to grow your confidence and intimate connection.

Growing your sexual confidence in sobriety will come with time. There might be awkward moments when you feel exposed, unsure, and vulnerable. But, as with anything, your confidence will grow as you continue to gain experience. If you take the initiative to educate yourself, practice, get curious, and even invest in modern sex ed for yourself or your partnership, I believe you will open yourself up to an entirely new world of sexual fulfillment and pleasure that you would have never thought possible as a drinker.

Romantic relationships tend to be our biggest opportunity for growth and expansion. Yet all relationships require work. Removing alcohol from the equation won't solve all your relationship problems. More realistically, it will allow you to see glaring problems you have been avoiding. I am proud of you for being brave enough to investigate the sacred mirror that your lovers hold up for you. I applaud you for taking the opportunity to grow from your relationships. If you are patient, persistent, and brave, changing your relationship with alcohol will undoubtedly open you up to more fulfilling romantic relationships and intimacy.

In the next chapter, we'll discover how to step into your potential in your most important relationship of all: your relationship with yourself.

CHAPTER 10

Living Your Most Authentic Life

Finding Personal Fulfillment through Being Yourself

> The sooner you step up into the greater most
> authentic version of You, the sooner your fears
> will dissipate, the sooner your concerns will begin
> to fade, the sooner life will bend towards you.
> The more you will flow with life.
>
> Rebecca Campbell, *Light Is the New Black*

One of the most important gifts I've ever received was from a man named Jeff, who I dated briefly after I turned thirty. Jeff was older, sophisticated, and devastatingly handsome. At the time, he was the Mr. Big to my Carrie Bradshaw. I admired and respected Jeff, so when he offered a gentle observation one night while driving home from dinner, I took notice. "Amanda," he said, "I feel like you're being . . . *calculated*." Wow. His comment felt harsh at first, but he wasn't wrong.

Unwittingly, I was indeed playing a carefully calculated role. I was constantly trying my best to be what I thought would earn me favor with others, and Jeff had called my bluff. For most of my life, I had been trying to be someone else. I obsessed over how to dress and act to make myself look cool. I was an expert chameleon who could magically transform into whomever I thought I was supposed to be in the moment. Eventually, I got so good at my act that I hardly realized I was frequently operating under a constructed persona.

Rather than be insulted by Jeff's comment, I somehow found the wherewithal to see it as an opportunity to grow. I promptly reenrolled in therapy and started devouring everything Brené Brown had ever written on the topics of vulnerability and authenticity. Once I committed to working on myself, it became abundantly clear that my calculated persona was more elaborate and ancient than I'd expected. I had effectively spent my twenties playing a part. I'd carefully crafted a character designed to accentuate the parts of myself that I felt would help me be what I perceived to be good, right, and popular. I also chose to conceal the parts of my persona that I judged as weird or different. The trouble is, when we cherry-pick our own innate traits, we lose our brilliance and uniqueness. Instead of shining brightly as the magnificent magical beings we were born to be, we dilute ourselves into a cheap facsimile, slowly becoming a one-dimensional version of who we were intended to be.

My conversation with Jeff was one of the major catalysts in my decision to become sober. Deep down, I knew that the person I became as a drinker was a diluted hologram of the person I was capable of being. Once I was turned on to the idea that I'd been hiding behind a facade, there was no turning back. I began to yearn to meet my authentic self and share her with the world. I knew this would be no small feat and that I certainly couldn't do it with alcohol in the way.

With alcohol out of the picture, I finally had the mental and emotional space to begin peeling back the armor I'd been hiding behind for decades. Although I'd spent countless hours agonizing about who I'd be as a nondrinker, I found that the woman I'd been hiding was quite incredible. In fact, she was infinitely more intriguing, entertaining, intelligent, and wonderful than she'd ever been as a drinker. You see, while I'd thought alcohol was bringing out the most desirable parts of my persona, it was only diluting my most charming and unique characteristics.

The world does not need a watered-down hologram of you. We ache for your authenticity and your brilliance. You were put here and uniquely programmed to be the weird, wonderful unicorn of a person that you are. Please do not, for one more moment, deprive us of that version of you.

I've come to believe that your highest function in this lifetime is to be authentically yourself. If you're like me and you've spent years trying to be someone other than yourself, you'll know how exhausting and heartbreaking it can feel to be disconnected from your authentic essence. Tapping back into your authenticity is much like how the great artist Michelangelo described sculpting David. Michelangelo did not envision sculpting David from a giant block of marble. Rather, he insisted that David was inside the block of marble all along. For over two years, Michelangelo made it his work to chip away at all that was not David, ultimately revealing a masterpiece. Are you like David, a masterpiece hidden under layers and layers of programming that have concealed your magnificence from our view? Make it your work to slowly chip away at anything that is not you so that your true form can be revealed.

Authenticity has become something of a buzzword over the last few years. There are certainly a lot of misrepresentations of the concept floating around on social media that are enough to make you cringe at the word. To help clarify what I mean by living authentically, let's turn back to the lessons of my first teacher on the topic, Brené Brown. In her book *The Gifts of Imperfection*, Brené says that authenticity is "the daily practice of letting go of who we think we're supposed to be and embracing who we are." Although there is no linear process for becoming authentic, I'll share some principles that have helped me along my journey as an alcohol-free woman.

AUTHENTICITY AND POTENTIAL

Authenticity is the backbone of achieving your potential. If you're not tapped into your authentic truth, it's likely you'll struggle with naming and claiming your genuine desires. To step fully into your potential, you have to know what you want . . . and you need the courage and confidence to go after it. Important aspects of achieving your potential include living out your dreams and desires, expressing your creativity, exploring hobbies, achieving personal goals, finding your calling, and connecting with your higher self. The simple truth is that most of us have gotten so caught up with the expectations of society that we've lost touch with what we want. We end up pursuing mediocre, average lives instead of pursuing our authentic desires.

When you lose touch with your authentic self and stop striving for your personal potential, it is common to experience discontent at best and depression at worst. Under the spell of discontent and depression, many people turn to a solution like alcohol to numb the pain and confusion.

A great example of this is my client Tessa, who grew up in a family where personal achievement was of the utmost importance. From a young age, Tessa was groomed academically and tutored in music. Her natural talents, combined with her top-notch education, positioned Tessa as a prodigy throughout her childhood and youth. When Tessa was a child, her parents made it clear that she was expected to be a high achiever.

When I met her, Tessa had a successful professional career and a list of talents that left me in absolute awe. To boot, Tessa is also one of the gentlest, kindest souls I've ever met. But under her kindness lived a layer of dormant frustration and confusion. Tessa shared that she felt tremendously privileged to live the life she lived. At the same time, she felt completely unsatisfied with her outwardly successful life. The combination of privilege and discontent left Tessa feeling guilty that she couldn't just find a way to be happy with the generous hand she'd been dealt in life.

When she came to me, Tessa had worked herself into such a state of misery and overwhelm, trying to keep up with the unrealistic expectations of her current reality, that she spent each night drowning her sorrows in wine. Although Tessa wasn't an alcoholic, she knew drinking was holding her back from being her most authentic self. It was preventing her from pursuing her dreams and desires by keeping her stuck in her current reality. At the end of the day, Tessa wanted nothing more than to feel at home in her body and have the time, energy, and confidence to fully pursue her passion for healing and spirituality.

Tessa's story is an example of how we can abandon our authentic selves along with our dreams and desires in favor of what others want for us. In Tessa's case, this included leaning into specific gifts and talents to meet her parents' expectations. It's also common to adapt our personalities to align with what we deem to be socially good, right, or popular. We've all abandoned different parts of our authentic nature, some more than others. In conscious individuals, it doesn't matter how much of your authentic self you've disconnected from or for what reason; you will eventually begin to ache and yearn to reconnect with that part of yourself.

In Tessa's case, she was so focused on making her family proud that she'd buried parts of herself that were essential to her soul's happiness. As a result, she felt caught in a professional rat race that, while rewarding on many levels, was so demanding that it left little time to fulfill her desire to express herself through hobbies and extracurricular activities she was passionate about. Because Tessa had been taught that exploring herself in this way was impermissible or even careless, she abandoned her desires and used alcohol as a coping mechanism for the huge levels of misalignment she felt.

Most of the women I work with tell me they, too, have abandoned, sacrificed, or downplayed their own needs and desires to meet the expectations of family or society at large. In most cases, the discomfort of misalignment eventually sinks in, and alcohol becomes a useful tool for anesthetizing the lingering discomfort of feeling personally unfulfilled. It only makes sense that we'd choose a coping mechanism like alcohol in times when we subconsciously seek to forget ourselves.

You might also relate to my client Maria. Maria is one of the most high-achieving, hardworking go-getters I've ever met. When we started working together, Maria was at the top of her game professionally and had a list of side hustles, social commitments, and volunteer activities that wore me out just looking at it. I often joked that I wanted to hire Maria because she's the type of lady who gets shit done.

Given all her professional achievements, it was no surprise that Maria had placed a great deal of importance on her career identity. She spent years climbing the professional ladder and was hanging on at the top for the promise of a handsome retirement package. There was only one problem. Even though Maria was awesome at her job, her career wasn't her passion or her calling. Maria had always dreamed of being an author, and she pitched me an inspiring idea for a book that I immediately knew she had to write. Maria's book had been on her heart for years, but she'd invested so much time in her current overscheduled identity that she hardly had time to start on a book. It came as no shock that Maria had also formed an alliance with alcohol. It was her tool for numbing herself through a litany of unfulfilling social events or shutting off the nagging voice that encouraged her to leap off the career ladder she'd devoted her life to climbing.

Get Clear on Your Core Values

If you're feeling misaligned with your current path, one of the most important activities you can do—outside of ditching alcohol, of course—is to get clear on your core values. Doing so will help you better understand how to set boundaries with yourself and others and know which opportunities to pursue and which to let pass you by without remorse.

When I completed my first core values exercise back in 2017, my values emerged as authenticity, happiness, love, peace, and spirituality. Decidedly, none of these values were present in my life as a drinker. I was hustling to achieve them, but every attempt seemed to fall short. When I looked at my daily life there was barely a whisper of authenticity, happiness, love, peace, or spirituality. What's worse, each and every quest to achieve these valued states had felt cumbersome at best and impossible at worst.

As I investigated the possible through lines that were keeping me from living out my core values, my intuition again led me to my relationship with alcohol. The unsettling reality was that the frequent influx of alcohol into my life kept me from having even a basic understanding of what it meant to act authentically, experience happiness, give or receive love, feel at peace, or establish a spiritual connection. One thing was clear: if I wanted to start living out these core values, I needed to start living differently.

Establish Your Core Values

Use this simplified list to select your core values. Start by selecting all that resonate with you and then narrow them down to three to five values. These values should serve as your guiding light for how you spend your time and who you spend it with.

Achievement	Autonomy	Challenge
Adventure	Balance	Citizenship
Authenticity	Beauty	Community
Authority	Boldness	Compassion

Competency	Inner Harmony	Recognition
Contribution	Justice	Religion
Creativity	Kindness	Reputation
Curiosity	Knowledge	Respect
Determination	Leadership	Responsibility
Fairness	Learning	Security
Faith	Love	Self-Respect
Fame	Loyalty	Service
Friendships	Meaningful Work	Spirituality
Fun	Openness	Stability
Growth	Optimism	Status
Happiness	Peace	Success
Honesty	Pleasure	Trustworthiness
Humor	Poise	Wealth
Influence	Popularity	Wisdom

This list of core values isn't exhaustive; you can do a quick Google search to find more examples or add values of your own that feel right. If you're having trouble, ask, What are the positive feelings I'd like to experience on a daily basis?

Once you've established your core values, you'll be able to weigh daily decisions against these values. Make a habit of asking, Do my current behaviors and relationships help me align with my values? If the answer is no, this is an invitation to reconsider those behaviors and relationships.

When choosing your values, remember that they are bound to change and evolve over time; they are not set in stone. You are a dynamic human being on a complex journey called life. Your relationships and desires are allowed—if not expected—to evolve.

For example, there was a time when the relationship with alcohol served you and your past core values system, even if you had not defined them. I believe drinking is a rite of passage in our culture. However, it's important to acknowledge that during your transition into adulthood, you had different values than you have now. As our values evolve, so, too, must the ways in which we show up in the world. If your relationship with alcohol is no longer serving the version of you that you are becoming, it's time to realign. Remember: You don't need to have a problem with alcohol for alcohol to be a problem in your life. The moment your relationship with alcohol causes misalignment with your current values, it becomes a problem.

EXPRESSING YOUR AUTHENTICITY AND PERSONAL POTENTIAL

I believe pursuing your personal potential is essential to your success as nondrinker. When you remove drinking from your agenda, you'll automatically free up time and energy that you can spend elsewhere. It's important that you find fulfilling ways to use this time so that you can experience the true benefit of being alcohol-free. It can be tempting to throw yourself into your current work or something you deem to be productive by societal standards, but I want to encourage you to be mindful of how you spend your newfound time and energetic freedom. Your personal potential includes pursuing things like rewarding hobbies and personal achievements you may have abandoned years ago. Or, perhaps you have an obscure list of "someday when" goals you haven't committed to pursuing. Now is the time. Tapping back into your authentic self and working to live out your personal potential might feel frivolous at first, but I can assure you that the payoff will be tremendously rewarding. Start by following my three-step method for getting into authentic alignment:

Step 1: **Be curious.** Because messages about authenticity on social media have become so convoluted, it can be difficult to understand exactly what authenticity is. Authenticity is often represented as being real, raw, and unfiltered; it's giving others a piece of our mind. (Picture literally any character from a reality TV show.) True authenticity is vulnerable and kind; it is offering others a bit of our heart. Early on in my journey, I decided to get curious about what it really means to be authentic. I sought out mentors I felt were doing it right and committed to learning from their wisdom. Some teachers who inspired me along my journey include Marianne Williamson, Glennon Doyle, Danielle LaPorte, Rebecca Campbell, Jessica Zweig, and Brené Brown. These women are brilliant authors and teachers, and I am deeply indebted to them for their teachings and encouragement.

Step 2: **Be friendly.** If we want to meet our authentic self, we must get friendly with all the versions of self that exist within us. Each has served a purpose in getting us to where we are today. One of my mentors, Eben, taught me how powerful it can be to look back at the past versions of yourself and honor them for how they have protected you and helped you grow into the next phase. Imperfect as they are, each past version of yourself has played an integral role in guiding you to where you are today. Their wisdom and experience are invaluable gifts to you.

Take a moment to consider all the past versions of yourself that have emerged, starting at the point when you began drinking. For example, I've been an Awkward Adolescent, a Party Girl, a Midwestern Carrie Bradshaw, a Sober-Curious Spiritual Seeker, and an Alcohol-Free Lifestyle Architect. (It's nice to give these past personas fun names.) Although there are aspects of my past personas that I no longer desire to hold on to, I have made a practice of befriending these past versions of me because without them, I wouldn't be the woman I am today.

If you'd like me to walk you through a formal exercise to meet and get friendly with your past selves, you can visit the resources webpage for this book: amandakuda.com/unbottledresources.

Step 3: **Be courageous.** It takes tremendous courage to show up for life without the masks you've been hiding behind or anything to numb you from the discomfort of vulnerability. It's not that you don't know how to be your authentic self; it's that you lack practice. You've spent years and years cheating the system, and now you must identify and unlearn all the suboptimal behaviors you've taken on and relearn a new way to get along in the world. Unlearning is the great work of authentic living, and it can help to find someone to support you in this endeavor. We all have blind spots and—by definition—they're incredibly difficult to see from your own point of view. Your blind spots are your coping mechanisms, challenges, and insecurities. They are your biggest areas of potential growth. Reading books like this one with a curious mind is a great way to get turned on to your blind spots. However, one of the most courageous moves you can make is enlisting the support of a therapist, coach, or mentor to assist you in uncovering your blind spots. Once we have the courage to show up and be real, we can let our truest, most authentic selves emerge.

REDEFINING PROFESSIONAL SUCCESS

I'm not sure how any of us were expected to create a comprehensive vision for our career trajectory as young adults. I am in awe of those of you who—by some combination of intuition, courage, and luck—managed to nail it on the first try. If you're like me, you know what it's like to spend years feverishly climbing a ladder only to become suspicious that you are, in fact, on the wrong ladder. If you, too, have been grappling with this realization, I want to share with you how removing alcohol from the picture can create the space and stability for you to leap off the wrong ladder and onto the right one.

For years, my vision of professional success was not mine, but one handed to me by society. I had my sights set on having an important job where I did important things and made loads of money. I took the necessary steps to achieve this vision by earning the right degrees and securing good jobs at good companies.

I realize now that my previous vision of professional success was based on a scarcity mentality, prestige, and societal norms. Climbing the corporate ladder was not my lifelong dream, but one I bought into because it was sold to me over and over as stable, sensible, and normal. This is not to say that pursuing a formal education or a traditional career path is bad or wrong, but to open space for you to redefine what professional success may look like for you.

Everybody Has a Calling

I believe that you came into this life with a calling—a purpose, a talent, a dream, a passion that you were meant to express. This calling might seem silly, frivolous, or impossible. It is yours, nonetheless. Your calling is your unique competitive edge. It's the thing that no one can do quite like you. When you are doing it, you feel at ease. This talent comes to you naturally. So much so that you rarely imagine it is anything special. It is. Your real work in this lifetime is to discover your calling and pursue it relentlessly. On some level, you know what this calling is, but you've likely spent so many years detached from it that it feels ancient and difficult to access.

It is not entirely necessary to pursue your calling in a professional nature. You may prefer to work a consistent job that affords you the opportunity to pursue your calling in other ways. However, if you choose this path, please be mindful that it will work best if your professional life yields a high payoff at a low level of stress.

Your Zone of Genius

I have no doubt that you are an intelligent and competent human being. If you're like most of my clients and me, you identify as a high performer and overachiever. You know how to get shit done, and you're naturally competent at a wide variety of things. You take pride in being able to conquer any challenge that is put in front of you.

However, this level of excellence also comes with heavy consequences. It's incredibly easy to get stuck in professional roles where you excel but aren't fulfilled. This paradigm is best explained by Gay Hendricks in his book *The Big Leap*. Hendricks shares that "our activities in the world occur in four main zones": the Zone of Incompetence ("all the activities we're not good at"), the Zone of Competence ("you're competent at the activities . . . but others can do them just as well"), the Zone of Excellence ("activities you do extremely well"), and the Zone of Genius ("activities you are uniquely suited to do").

Hendricks teaches that the Zone of Excellence is particularly seductive for extremely successful people as it can tempt them to remain there rather than make the leap into the Zone of Genius. Society at large wants you to stay in your Zone of Excellence because it is safe and reliable. However, Hendricks posits that a "deep, sacred part of you will wither and die if you stay inside your Zone of Excellence." Ultimately, alcohol can keep you stuck there.

Finding Your Calling

I don't expect you to clearly know your calling by the time you finish this chapter. Keep in mind that getting back to your authentic self will take time and may require some trial-and-error exploration. In my case, my calling presented itself to me slowly and divinely over the course of a couple of years. It's likely that you've always known what you were supposed to do but abandoned that dream and desire to pursue something that felt more practical or financially advantageous.

If you're ready to step into your professional potential but aren't sure of the next steps, here is a list of questions to set you on the right path:

If you're honest with yourself, do you feel your current career is your calling?

If so, what are your biggest aspirations within your career?

If you were to dream big—with no limitations, such as time, money, or experience—what is it that you would be paid to do?

What comes so easily to you that you couldn't imagine someone paying you to do it?

What topics most interest you? What could you spend hours getting lost in learning about?

In what areas do people come to you for help, advice, support, or guidance?

What were your dream careers as a child and adolescent? Do these paths still interest you? Is there a more sophisticated expression of this career available in the world today?

For example, I dreamed of being a teacher, but the only models I had as a child were my schoolteachers. Today, I *do* teach, but how I teach as a coach is different from anything I could have imagined as a child.

Take Small Steps

Make a list of small steps you can take to educate yourself further on pursuing your calling. Start with doing your own research. If you're unsure of what your calling is, the best way to find it is to become a curious learner. Read books and listen to podcasts about various career paths to broaden your view of what is possible. When I was preparing to leave my corporate job, I spent my spare time listening to entrepreneurial podcasts that introduced me to career paths I never would have considered a possibility. I constantly found myself saying, Wow, you can get paid for that? Sure enough, if you have a special talent, someone is out there looking for you to guide or support them.

If you have a strong feeling about your calling, start to get familiar with people who are already doing what it is that you desire. You can find these people through a Google search or on Instagram or LinkedIn. Connect with them, but take some time to lurk around before reaching out to them so that you're not asking questions you could have found the answer to easily. Keep an eye out for opportunities to learn from or with the individuals you've been admiring from afar. Consider investing in a course or service they offer. If they don't offer a way to work with them, then take the next step and reach out to them.

As you gain more exposure to possibilities, it's likely that your vision for expressing your calling will evolve. Do the groundwork, but trust in divine timing and follow your intuition toward new connections and opportunities that may guide you closer to your calling. Continuing to take tiny steps in the direction of your calling can lead to a big transformation. During our time working together, I'm able to support the majority of my high-level private clients into a massive career transition or promotion once alcohol is out of the way. It is my belief that the world needs the special magic that you have. I'm always delighted to hear how deciding to become sober has helped my clients and students share their magic with the world.

CONNECTING WITH YOUR HIGHER SELF AND A HIGHER POWER

I've never been a particularly religious person. I grew up in the Midwest and spent my young adulthood in the Bible Belt of Missouri, where the tenets of religion were very inflexible. This level of rigidity never resonated with me (not to mention that my Party Girl lifestyle was in no way considered holy). Even as a child, I was not interested in the dogma of traditional religion. Nevertheless, I always remember feeling connected to a power outside my physical sight. As a young girl, I frequently communicated with this entity before falling asleep or when life felt hectic.

It wasn't until my late twenties that I realized it was possible to cultivate a spiritual relationship of my own understanding. Suddenly, my world expanded, and I began yearning for a spiritual connection that would give me the sense of inner peace that I read about in spiritual self-help books.

There was only one problem. Even though I cultivated a life of mindfulness on weekdays, I dedicated my weekends to being entirely mindless out on the social scene. I became spiritually curious a few years ahead of becoming sober curious, but as desperate as I was to have the best of both worlds, it was a struggle to maintain these two opposing lifestyles.

When I look back at my camera roll from those years, I see the face of a young woman in the midst of an awakening but terrified to step fully into the transformation available to her. The photos in my phone alternate between screenshots of spiritual quotes and personal growth books I was reading and images of me donning a performative, open-mouthed smile, cocktail raised high in the air, eyes distant and glossed over.

On one hand, I wanted to hold on to the life that was familiar, even though it was slightly unsatisfying. Staying where I was would allow me to maintain the persona I worked so tirelessly to build. On the other hand, I wanted to disappear into nothingness and reemerge like a butterfly after metamorphosis.

Of all the feats I tried to accomplish as a Party Girl, tapping into a spiritual connection was by far the most difficult and frustrating. No matter how many spiritual texts I read, meditations I completed, retreats I attended, or prayers I prayed, it still seemed like I wasn't fully connecting with this all-loving presence that others seemed to find so profound. It's as if I was seeing and hearing the words, but my brain was not fully computing the message.

As time passed, I began to ache more intensely for this spiritual connection. I longed to experience the sense of knowing and connectedness that my spiritual mentors described. I felt, in the depths of my soul, that this connection was meant to be mine and that I would never fully access it if I insisted on clinging to the security blanket that was alcohol.

Perhaps you, too, have been experiencing this gentle nudge but feel caught in the double bind of pursuing the life you desire while simultaneously clinging to the life you have worked hard to create. In my work as a coach, I have found that spiritual curiosity and sober curiosity are often collaborators in exploring your potential. If you've found these two curiosities appearing in your life at once, I believe it is no coincidence.

Sobriety and Spiritual Awakenings

When I first gave up drinking, I thought it was because I no longer liked the way alcohol made me feel, which was true. But as I look back now, it's abundantly clear that I was also on the cusp of a massive spiritual awakening, and all the intense physical hangovers, the mental anxiety, and the curiosity about sobriety were cues sent to me by my Inner Guide who knew—without question—that alcohol was blocking me from my connection to the Universe.

If this resonates with you, let me share some characteristics of a spiritual awakening and why it might be fueling your desire to quit drinking:

- A feeling of disconnection/differentness from friends and family

- An increasing discontent with mundane social activities and small talk

- An awareness that you have a unique way of seeing the world that may have caused you to feel distant from others throughout your life

- A sense of knowing that you are meant for something more

- A strong desire to go inward, to be alone

- An increased sensitivity to drama and pettiness

- A newfound sense of openness to ideas and mindsets that you once brushed off as "out there"

- An anticipated grief over the loss of who you were, the version you worked so hard to manufacture

- An unshakable yearning for a more meaningful life experience

- A desire to meet and embrace your authentic self

Essentially, a spiritual awakening is an unshakable internal desire for an energetic upgrade. As you can see from the examples above, it's as if your body and mind stop being attracted to and tolerant of the mundane. This doesn't mean we should dip out of society and avoid modern conveniences altogether. Rather, it's a sacred invitation to invest more energy in the activities that fill us up.

This is not about whether it is right or wrong to drink. It is about if alcohol is serving you or blocking you from living the life you are capable of. Call it what you want: spiritual awakening, soul awakening, existential crisis, mid- or quarter-life crisis, identity crisis, or metamorphosis. No matter how you slice it, I've met individuals from all stages of life and a variety of backgrounds who have an increasing urge to change their relationship with alcohol as part of a bigger life transformation. These people have been called to explore and express a higher level of potential, and deep inside they know alcohol is holding them back.

But if you're like I was, stepping into a spiritual path can feel overwhelming, particularly if you've also become somewhat disenchanted with—or even skeptical of—traditional religion. A quick spin around your social media platform of choice will expose you to a wide range of spiritual and metaphysical practices.

Spirituality is what you make of it, but ultimately, it's the willingness to tap into ancient wisdom within yourself. You need nothing outside of yourself to be a spiritual person. You don't need to subscribe to a particular religious affiliation, follow a guru, collect crystals, read tarot, go on a retreat, sit in meditation, ingest psychedelics, or practice yoga to be considered spiritual. Sure, your spiritual practice can include any or all of these things. It might not include any of them at all. There are no requirements to identify as "spiritual" because you are inherently a spiritual being. Or, as spiritual teacher Wayne Dyer puts it, "We are not human beings having a spiritual experience; we are spiritual beings having a human experience." In other words, there is an omnipresent spiritual connection within us all; we just allow our human experience to overshadow it.

When it comes to spirituality, society has failed us by trying to force-feed us religious dogma, trendy approaches to being woke, or pleas to be ruthlessly self-reliant. Although I have found my own approach to spirituality, just a few years ago I was intimidated to explore and share my spiritual side with others.

Aside from my decision to quit drinking, my spiritual connection has undoubtedly been the most important element of my lived potential. I believe it was my spiritual curiosity that drove me toward exploring an alcohol-free lifestyle. Likewise, it was my decision to become alcohol-free that opened me up to a meaningful spiritual connection. They are profoundly supportive of one another.

My spiritual practice has allowed me to heal from the past and release expectations about the future. Spirituality has fundamentally improved the way I show up in this world. The shifts that have occurred in my life through the combination of spirituality and sobriety are nothing short of profound. Therefore, I invite you to consider tapping into your spiritual potential as an opportunity to find infinite support in your own life.

Going Down the Spiritual Rabbit Hole

I believe the most productive spiritual connections are those we cultivate using intuition. You can cultivate a spiritual connection of your own understanding, and I encourage you to do so.

As you delve into spiritual practice, you might be drawn to explore a multitude of approaches, teachers, practices, and tools. I invite you to become a curious learner. Remember, your intuition is here to guide you; lean into the ideas and teachers that resonate most with you, and use them as a springboard for your spiritual exploration.

Explore spiritual teachers and texts. Take the time to dip your toe into the spiritual pond and learn from a variety of teachers to find the approaches and messages that most resonate with you. Let yourself go down the rabbit hole of spirituality and find what speaks to your soul.

I find podcasts are a great place to start, as various hosts will exercise due diligence to expose listeners to a variety of teachers with different areas of expertise and focus. Much of my early exposure came from Oprah Winfrey, who has interviewed many of the most profound spiritual thought leaders of our time. My typical process for going down a rabbit hole of spiritual practice is to find a teacher I resonate with and search that person's name in my podcast app. I'll then listen to them speak on other podcasts, and if there's a podcast host I resonate with, I'll dig in and listen to more episodes of their show, which often leads me to new findings to explore. Some of my favorite podcasts for becoming exposed to spiritual teachers include *Expanded, Almost 30, Good Life Project*, and *The Life Stylist*.

Journal. If you haven't caught on to this yet, I am a big fan of journaling as a form of personal development and healing. Something special happens when you put physical pen onto paper and let your words flow through. I love journaling as a way to connect with your Inner Guide and to a spiritual presence of your own understanding. (I frequently use the terms "Spirit" or "the Universe" to describe this presence. You can substitute any term that works best for you.) Often, the pages of my journal are filled with prayers or letters to the Universe as I process what is happening in my life. I find the act of communicating with the Universe through writing to be extremely soothing. I also like the idea that my communication has been clearly documented. After it's in writing, I have no doubt that my request for support has been received, so I find it much easier to stop obsessing over the outcome.

Every so often, I enjoy revisiting my journals with a highlighter in hand to observe and appreciate my growth and take in the quantity of my prayers that have been answered. This practice cultivates an overwhelming feeling of gratitude and reminds me I am always being supported.

Pray. Prayer is nothing more than a sacred space where you can communicate with Spirit. There is no right or wrong way to pray. As I just shared, I often write my own prayers in my journal, but I also have a spoken prayer practice where I allow the words to come to me in real time.

The practice of allowing prayer to flow through me has taken time to cultivate. In my early days, my prayers felt clunky and slow. Even when I was praying alone, I felt as if the words weren't quite coming together as I would have liked. Let me assure you, eloquence is not required for the message to get through.

I look at prayer as a way to share with the Universe what I am challenged with and to invite Spirit to intervene with a solution that is of the highest good for all. Therefore, I try my best not to be too controlling or needy with my prayers. This was a significant challenge for me as a recovering control freak and know-it-all. Today, I trust that the Universe knows what is best for me and has a line of sight that I do not quite yet have. My goal in prayer is to turn over my issue to Spirit and release the outcome to a higher power.

It's important to remember that while you are always being supported and guided, you also have free will. This means that Spirit cannot interfere with or manipulate you or your surroundings without your clear permission. This is why prayer is important: it is your spoken or written invitation to the Universe.

If you're like me as a beginner, the prayer practice might feel awkward at first. One way I became more comfortable with prayer was to listen and watch as others modeled the practice for me. I'd sink in and listen as my teachers and mentors offered up prayers during their recorded and live lectures. Listening to prayers from more seasoned spiritual leaders allowed me to create my own style of prayer and feel more comfortable with the overall process.

Meditate. Meditation comes in many forms. It does not require you to sit cross-legged near the peak of a mountain with your eyes gently closed, quietly humming "Om." Although there is great value in learning to sit in silence and allow your thoughts to simply be, meditation for you might look like a silent walk in nature, losing yourself in dance, or creating a beautiful painting. Many of your everyday activities can become meditative if you approach them with intention. Recently, one of my spiritual teachers shared how she uses laundry time as a meditative practice—you can do this with any routine activity you find cathartic.

Frequently, my most meditative experiences are found when walking or sitting silently in nature. When I first started writing this book, I was invited by my dear friend Melissa to stay at her cottage in Southern California. The cottage had a small backyard shaded by a fragrant mimosa tree. The tree attracted birds of all kinds throughout the day, and some of my most beautiful periods of meditation were found lying on the ground under the tree, watching the birds come and go.

When I was getting started with meditation, I found it most helpful to begin with very short increments and work my way up to longer time frames. I found my tolerance for unguided meditation was rather short in the beginning, but my resilience to sitting grew over time. Early on, the meditations I found particularly helpful were guided by experienced teachers who would offer verbal cues for breathing, visualization, or inspiration. My favorite app for meditation is Insight Timer because of the variety of teachers and meditation styles available on the platform, but you might also enjoy Calm, Headspace, or one of the other popular options available right on your phone.

Practice breathwork. Breathwork has become a buzzword in the spiritual community over the last few years, and it's no wonder why. I've found the various available breathwork practices to be tremendously powerful and transformative. As with meditation, there are multiple forms of breathwork practice, all of which center around maintaining various breathing patterns. To start exploring breathwork practices, consider the guided sessions available on one of the apps I mentioned above, or check out a live breathwork session in your area.

I've found that breathwork can be extremely powerful once you find a format, environment, and teacher you resonate with. In early 2021, I went on a beautiful retreat where our resident yogi and breathwork teacher, Rebecca, guided our group through a magical breathwork session during which I experienced a cathartic emotional release. Throughout the session, I felt the crescendo of the music tracks wash over me. Several times, I was overwhelmed with the urge to wail and sob as though I were in intense physical pain, even though I was feeling physically relaxed. At one point, I felt the presence of an angel adorned in blue silks hovering over me. She kneeled, placed a hand on my shoulder, and began pulling thick, heavy ropes from my right shoulder. The ropes eventually turned into dark blue silks, matching her outfit, which she fanned in the air before draping them over me. This experience was powerful, emotional, and completely transformative. It was a naturally psychedelic experience where the only healing power present was that of my own breath.

While it might sound easy to do on your own, I highly recommend you try to find an in-person event for your first breathwork experience. Because you'll move a lot of energy, which can be a highly emotional experience, it's nice to have a teacher to facilitate and hold space for your experience. If this is not available in your area, you'll find plenty of guided sessions across various meditation apps.

My desire for you is that you become the person you are capable of being. This cannot be accomplished if you consume your time trying to become someone you are not. This is precisely what we all do as drinkers. We use alcohol to perform and transform. We use alcohol to forget the parts of ourselves we find unlovable or imperfect. You are being called to come home to yourself. You are being called to stop escaping and diluting yourself. You are being called to stand in the vulnerable yet fulfilling space that is living authentically. It is from this space that you will be able to hold sacred the emotions you once tried to stifle, connect more intimately with others, and tap into your Zone of Genius. You deserve this level of connectedness in your life.

In the next chapter, we'll take a look at some of the common stumbling blocks you're bound to encounter along your journey of changing your relationship with alcohol. I'll help you identify some sneaky forms of self-sabotage to be on the lookout for and arm you with tools to keep your momentum and resist temptation so that you can step into your potential with as much ease as possible.

CHAPTER 11

Potential Stumbling Blocks

Getting Past Common Temptations and Self-Sabotage

The hard part is going against groupthink,
the herd mentality of our alcohol-saturated culture.
After all, alcohol is the only drug on earth you
have to justify *not* taking.

Annie Grace, *This Naked Mind*

In my work as a coach, it doesn't bother (or surprise) me when one of my clients calls to confess that they've had a slipup with alcohol. I don't even like to refer to these occurrences as *slipups, mistakes,* or *relapses.* These are minor stumbling blocks, or as I prefer to call them: *learning opportunities.* In my experience as a coach, the only mistake is the lesson we choose not to learn. Changing your relationship with alcohol is going to be a journey filled with many opportunities to learn and grow. I, for one, am proud of you for choosing to show up and learn the lesson.

Before we get started with the lessons in this chapter, it's important that you understand that you are not a failure or bad person for stumbling along the way; you are human. Furthermore, you are a human working to rewire and reimagine a long-term, seductive relationship with a substance that has made you many shallow promises. You are working not only to change a behavior that you've most likely been playing out for decades but also to rewire a series of thoughts that have been ingrained in your subconscious for much longer than that. It's only rational to bet that you might stumble along the way or find it enticing to go back to the old way. You may have days when you are tired and fed up, days when your willpower is weak, days when everything is absolutely glorious, or days when you feel like sobriety is a brutal punishment.

The journey of healing and growth is not an upward, linear climb but a twisting and turning roller coaster. Ups and downs are normal and expected; I want you to have the tools to be prepared for them. Along the way, your resilience and commitment will be challenged and tested in both sneaky and obvious ways. The purpose of this chapter is to alert you to the many ways you might be tempted to self-sabotage and what to do if and when that temptation strikes.

BEWARE OF THE PINK CLOUD

There's a phenomenon in the sobriety world known as the "pink cloud." It's a state of euphoria and bliss that often appears in individuals who have removed alcohol from their lives. There's no set timeline for when the pink cloud may appear, but rest assured, if you break up with booze and follow the steps outlined in this book to break through to your best life and start living to your potential, you are bound to experience your own version of the pink cloud.

Although this experience is wonderful, I want to alert you that the pink cloud can also serve as a sneaky precursor to the perfect storm. As twisted as it sounds, feeling good can be intimidating to your nervous system. As you learned in chapter 7, embracing positive, high-vibe emotions might feel awkward or overwhelming if you've been living in a world where your nervous system is constantly dysregulated by alcohol. This is compounded by the fact that many of us have been conditioned to be on high alert for the other shoe to drop when things start to get good. Therefore, when you start to feel good, your Inner Critic goes into sabotage mode and schemes ways to divert you from this good feeling.

In my private coaching practice, I keep track of some of the most common areas where the euphoria of the pink cloud can turn into temptation. Take a look at these examples, and make a note to be on the lookout for the sneaky ways your Inner Critic might attempt to sabotage your success.

The temptation of reward. If you've been busting through alcohol-free milestones and overcoming obstacles left and right, it's likely that your Inner Critic will eventually try to persuade you to have a drink as a reward for all your hard work. If you're tempted to reward yourself, the dialogue of your Inner Critic will go something like this: You've been working so hard. You've been so good. You deserve to cut loose and treat yourself to one drink. You can do it just this once.

My client Fiona learned her lesson with rewards early on in her sober journey. Through our work together, Fiona was able to achieve her longest stint of abstinence yet. She'd reached sixty days and felt so proud and empowered before her Inner Critic crept in to tempt her. Although she'd managed to survive several other big occasions alcohol-free, it was a celebratory event that tempted Fiona to break her streak for one night as a reward for being so diligent. The next morning, her decision to drink hardly felt like a reward. Hung over and feeling defeated, Fiona messaged me to share how frustrated she was with herself.

If you're tempted to reward yourself with a drink along the way, remember this: no true reward comes with a punishment.

In my humble opinion, a hangover coupled with self-loathing is a punishment of the worst kind.

Being on the brink of success. It's often when you are riding high that your Inner Critic will pop in and do a doozy on your self-confidence. Maybe you've been given a promotion at work, or a big dream of yours has come to fruition. It is on these days you might be most tempted to indulge in a drink to celebrate. Make no mistake, the allure of celebration is actually disguising your Inner Critic's master plan to sabotage your happiness.

My client Kali is a perfect example of this. Kali is extremely intelligent and incredibly successful in her career. When we began working together, she'd just received a major accolade in her industry and had been given several new opportunities as a result. On one of our visits, Kali told me she suspected she was about to receive another significant industry recognition. Her eyes beamed with pride as she delivered this news.

One week later, I received a voice note from Kali. She told me she'd broken her sobriety streak on a night out with coworkers. She had a clumsy accident after a drunken night out, but what was wounded most was her pride. When we debriefed, I asked Kali bluntly if she believed she deserved to be happy. Her eyes filled with tears, and she confessed that despite how respected and successful she was at her job, she often felt like a fraud.

Deep down, many of us crave success, but we don't believe we are deserving of it. So instead of expanding into the feeling of success when it comes along (because it will), we shut down and contract, unable to hold space for our own magnificence. We drink to reinforce the tiny negative voice inside that causes us to question ourselves and our worthiness. Choosing to drink as a pseudocelebration for our success guarantees that our burst of joy and confidence will not last. Sometimes we do this to the extent that we end up compromising our success, thus proving to ourselves that we are not worthy. In Kali's case, she came *this close* to embarrassing herself in front of higher-ups in the industry she was so desperately trying to succeed in.

Enhancing beautiful days. One of the most common reasons for slipups in my clients is the presence of a beautiful day or experience. You know the scene: the sun is shining or you're at the lake or in the mountains or overlooking an epic vista, and it seems like a perfect day for a glass of crisp chardonnay, a salty margarita, or a cold pint out on the patio.

It can be tempting to indulge in your favorite beverage as a way to, as my clients like to put it, "add to the experience" of a beautiful day or enjoy a good view. But does dulling your senses to beauty *really* add to the experience? Of course it doesn't. You know by now that drinking numbs your senses and keeps you from being fully present in the moment. Yet time and time again, my clients and students are tempted by this simple trick of their Inner Critic.

I like to think of drinking on a good day as a massive insult to Mother Nature. It's as if you're saying, Wow, this is gorgeous! But here, let me make it so that I can't experience it fully. Rather than succumbing to the desire to "enhance your experience" of a beautiful day with alcohol, I encourage you to go back to the Five Senses Meditation from chapter 6. Stop to appreciate the beauty you have in front of you, and find gratitude for your ability to experience it fully.

Testing the waters. At some point along your journey, you'll find yourself hitting a sobriety milestone such as ninety days, six months, or a year. Yay! I'm so proud of you! These occasions can be tricky as they often create irrational urges to test the waters. You'll rationalize that you've made it [insert length of time] without drinking and that by now, you should be fine . . . right?

My client Molly achieved more than six months of being alcohol-free. Feeling confident in her new lifestyle, Molly and I concluded our work together and agreed to check in regularly. Less than a year later, I saw an appointment for Molly on my calendar with a note that she'd decided to test the waters only to find herself right back where she'd started a few months earlier. Molly felt defeated and frustrated to be back in the same cycle she'd invested time and money to get out of.

This itch to test the waters is completely normal, yet rarely productive to scratch. The allure to test the waters is the Inner Critic's nasty trick to throw you off course and cause you to lose momentum on your journey. When temptation strikes, I encourage you to revisit the exercises from the prior chapters (particularly chapters 6 and 7) and remember, above all, that you deserve to be happy. You are deserving of happiness, bliss, and joy. These emotional experiences are your birthright and are intended to be your default state. Often, happiness can feel too good to be true or even overwhelming to handle. It feels good to feel good, but it can also feel scary to feel good. Do not allow your fear to outweigh your potential for happiness. Do not be fooled into believing that one moment of disconnection will add to your happiness in any way. Succumbing to the temptation to drink may allow you to have a momentary buzz, but sooner or later, that buzz will fade, leaving you with the same dismal, gray feeling that alcohol has always left you with.

Overdoing it. Most of my clients and students identify as go-getters. If this sounds like you, too, you've probably been operating at an unbelievably high capacity, even with alcohol in the picture. If so, you may be shocked when you reveal an entirely untapped level of time and energy available to you as a non-drinker. You may be tempted to fill up your calendar with activities and next steps for life goals that were previously on hold. I get it; you have big goals, dreams, and aspirations, and getting alcohol out of the way feels like the gateway to an entirely new life. This is your reminder to take it slow.

Learn from my client Lee, who unintentionally got herself into a bit of a pickle when she started feeling the euphoria of the pink cloud. Lee had tried to ditch alcohol several times, and deciding to work with me was the accelerant she needed to commit to her success. Lee shared that this break from alcohol felt different; it felt easy. We created a few simple goals for Lee to focus on in addition to being alcohol-free.

Two months into our work together, Lee confessed that she was exhausted. As it turns out, Lee had taken all our assignments to the next level, packing her calendar full of wellness activities to the point that she eventually overexerted herself. Lee admitted that the overwhelm from trying to do too much too fast almost tempted her to fall off track with her one main goal: living an alcohol-free life.

Lee's experience is not uncommon. It might seem like a great idea to throw yourself into hyperdrive once you start to experience the pink cloud. Be aware of the temptation to overdo it. Remember that you are still in a tender rebuilding period where your body is recalibrating and you are learning to embrace new emotions and experiences.

I know that for capable high achievers, striving for only the basics might seem like slacking. It's not. It's called self-care, and as you strengthen yourself through practicing the basics, you'll create more bandwidth to optimize your life in other ways.

As you acclimate to this new way of being, I recommend that you remove one suboptimal variable at a time, starting with alcohol. Once you have your first sixty days under your belt, evaluate what other negative habits you might want to remove and assess if you feel grounded enough to make any additional moves. When you are ready, remove additional variables one at a time as well.

Likewise, resist the temptation to go all in on adding positive habits to your day. This is not the time to become a biohacker or extreme athlete. Focus on adding in one positive variable at a time, giving yourself a minimum of two to four weeks to acclimate to new routines before adding in anything else.

An easy guideline is to add and remove variables in increments of twenty-one to thirty days, thoughtfully assessing your progress as you go. When my clients are in doubt, I remind them that there are only five basic requirements for each day: hydration, movement, sunshine (or outdoor time, even if it's overcast), nutrition, and rest. These basic components are the foundation for keeping your nervous system regulated. Even after years of practice, I find that on days when I feel dysregulated or anxious, I have inevitably slacked on one of these five basics.

Changing your relationship with alcohol can be the foundation for nearly any other positive change you want to make in your life. It is through this change that you can create new space to optimize, improve, and heal other aspects of your life. Please, be patient and gentle with yourself. Overexerting yourself is grounds for frying your nervous system (yes, even if you're throwing yourself into feel-good wellness activities). Although you might have the best of intentions, overdoing it can lead to overwhelm. Overwhelm can lead to the temptation to numb. I've seen many well-intentioned, capable women have a slipup with alcohol because they used the pink cloud effect to legitimize throwing themselves into new routines too quickly.

WHAT TO DO ON GRAY DAYS

It goes without saying that if you can be tempted to drink on pink cloud days, you'll also encounter a gray day when it is equally enticing to say "Screw it" and have a drink. There will be days when chaos ensues, emotions are high, or tragedy strikes. These days will happen, and they can blindside you and attempt to completely detour you from your path.

There will be days that feel heavy and insurmountable—days when you want nothing more than to escape your body and mind. These are the days when it is most important to stay the course. These are the days when you most need to show up for yourself and the world around you. These are the days when sobriety becomes your ally, even though it can feel like a punishment.

The days that feel gray and heavy will only become heavier if you attempt to numb and check out. Drinking is like pouring gasoline on anxiety or any other heavy emotion. You are no good to yourself or others if you choose to light yourself on fire.

I'm sharing this message just days after multiple tragic gun-violence events here in the United States. Over the past few days, I've had clients and students reach out to me with shaky voices and heavy hearts, confessing how tempted they were to drink to numb the unrest and heartbreak weighing on them. If you find yourself in this place, here is an excerpt from a message I shared with my email list following these tragedies:

> *It is in times like this that the world most needs you awake.*
>
> *Please, if you can, resist the urge to check out and shut down. You are more powerful when fueled by emotion than when you are numb. We need you at full capacity; that is where your power lies.*
>
> *If you feel you must numb, I understand and would never shame you for that choice. Yet I encourage you to consider other options, if you can.*
>
> *I honor you and any emotions that you are feeling right now. I honor your bravery to feel and be with them; I know it is not easy. Keep going.*

Some days it will feel like a punishment to have chosen sobriety. It may feel like you're not making fast enough progress or that life has gotten worse, not better. On these days, I encourage you to refer to the tools I shared in chapter 7 for embracing your emotions. I encourage you to be willing and brave enough to do the great work of showing up for yourself and staying the course of pursuing your potential. In the likely event of gray days ahead, use these simple principles as a guide:

Be gentle with yourself. In the event that you stumble or fall off the wagon, be gentle with yourself. You are a human being having a human experience. You are imperfect, and there will be days when you disappoint yourself. Resist the urge to beat yourself up; you deserve grace and forgiveness, most of all from yourself.

Choose to learn the lesson. Avoid the temptation to let a mistake turn into a downward spiral. If you've fallen off the wagon, get back on and get curious about what you were actually looking for when you made the decision to break your commitment to sobriety. Were you secretly attempting to sabotage your happiness and success? Or were you seeking a type of relief or connection you were too impatient to give to yourself?

Avoid the comparison trap. It's been said "comparison is the thief of joy." Comparing your life story to someone else's highlight reel is a recipe for disaster. It may appear that other people have it easier than you when it comes to their sobriety journey or life in general. Remember that you never know what someone is experiencing behind closed doors.

Things get real before they get better. I'm sure you've heard the old adage "things get worse before they get better." Well, when it comes to sobriety, it might appear that things in your life are getting worse as a result of your new lifestyle. The reality is, things aren't getting worse; they're just getting real. You've been numbing yourself to the bleak reality around you, and now, with your senses and emotions on full alert, you are faced with the reality you've been avoiding. And yet you are more capable than you give yourself credit for. You have the capacity to deal with whatever life has thrown or will throw at you. This doesn't mean it will be easy, and I don't recommend you do it alone.

Take, for example, my client Deborah, who was on the front lines during the worst of the COVID-19 pandemic. Deborah frequently used alcohol to cope with the very real and disturbing experiences of her job. Deborah's trauma was real and raw. Even though she had the support of mental health professionals to help her cope with this trauma, she confessed, "If I'm being honest, I keep drinking because I'm not ready to go back there and deal with the reality of everything that happened."

What Deborah had not been able to see was that by drinking to repress her emotions, she wasn't avoiding going *back there*. Rather, she was perpetually keeping herself *stuck there*. When I lovingly shared this observation with Deborah, I saw a spark of relief and bravery in her eyes. She hadn't considered that the very thing she was using to avoid her trauma was the exact thing that was keeping her stuck in it. That day, Deborah committed to reaching out to her therapist and scheduling the necessary time to process the heavy emotions she'd been holding on to.

Whether you find yourself dealing with the reality of big-T Traumas, micro-traumas, or repressed grief, anger, or any other seemingly insurmountable emotion, please know that using alcohol as a coping mechanism is only a temporary and entirely ineffective solution. These life experiences typically don't get worse before they get better; they just get real.

It is also possible that the realities you are avoiding seem simple or petty to you in comparison to Deborah's experience or the experiences of others around you; do not let that make your healing any less important. Whatever the weight you've been carrying, this is your invitation to lift it from your shoulders in a way that feels safe and freeing. If you are unsure of your ability to face and process reality on your own, please do yourself the service of enlisting a support team to help you. My clients have found traditional talk therapy or more advanced therapeutic practices, including somatic processing, Internal Family Systems (IFS), Eye Movement Desensitization and Reprocessing (EMDR), and Ketamine Assisted Psychotherapy (KAP) treatments, to be tremendously helpful on their healing journeys. These therapeutic practices, combined with working with an experienced coach, can be powerful tools for transformative healing.

You deserve to heal. Staying stuck in the dullness of an uncomfortable reality is no way to live, and it will certainly not serve you in pursuing your potential.

The world needs you awake. Now, more than ever, the world needs you awake. We need you operating at full capacity. We need you showing up as your most healed, capable, vibrant self. We need you showing up to your fullest potential, holding space for your own experience and serving as a way-shower for others. Your openness to experiencing life from this perspective can and will elevate the frequency of the world around you. You have no idea how profoundly your choice to show up will shape the world.

Your bravery to show up for your life fully undiluted will directly affect your sense of self-esteem. Through your willingness to show up for life wholeheartedly, you will become more confident in your ability to cope. Over time, your confidence will grow, and being fully awake will begin to feel like your biggest triumph.

How to Keep Momentum and Resist Temptation

In the moments when you face seemingly irresistible temptation and want to throw your hands up and say "Screw it!" it's important that you have a practice for pausing to reflect before taking action. Here are some questions to ask yourself on the occasion that temptation arises:

What discomfort am I avoiding right now?

Is abandoning my goal really the way to honor my discomfort?

What do I really need right now?

Do I believe I am worthy and capable of having the thing I need?

Do I have the tools to give myself what I need?

Will drinking right now really help . . . or am I merely trying to escape discomfort?

How will I feel tomorrow if I compromise on this commitment I've made to myself?

When you feel temptation arise, the best thing you can do is take a moment to sit with your thoughts and emotions before deciding to act. Remember, your actions are driven by thoughts and feelings, many of which are subconscious. Therefore, you'll feel much more confident about a decision if you take a moment to consciously unpack your thoughts and assess your emotions.

WAKING UP

Waking up to your potential is big work. In the chapters of this book, I've outlined the simple first steps you can take to walk away from alcohol and toward your potential. I want to remind you that taking the initiative to do this work is imperative to your success. I've coached many clients who have done the important work of removing alcohol from their lives but avoided the necessary work of uncovering and healing the why behind their relationship with alcohol.

A great example is my client Nell, who achieved more than six years of being alcohol-free before deciding to test the waters of integrating alcohol back into her life. Before too long, Nell recounted that she was right back to her old drinking habits and felt like she'd flushed six years of abstinence down the drain. As we dove into our work together, I learned that Nell's primary tactic for changing her relationship with alcohol was to abstain. She hadn't engaged in therapy or coaching or done much more than reading a few basic self-help books. It made perfect sense to me that Nell might revert to her old habit because she'd never investigated the thoughts and feelings that were driving the habit.

It's common among my clients to get swept up by the euphoria of the pink cloud. With your newfound energy and zest for life, you might find yourself tempted to fill your time with activities that society has deemed productive or to distract yourself with social activities or new hobbies and obsessions. Of course, I want you to explore new passions and use your glorious pink cloud energy to pursue your goals and fulfill your potential. Please do not do this at the expense of your emotional growth and healing. Avoid the urge to use productivity and achievement to avoid doing the very important and often uncomfortable yet tremendously freeing work that will best set you up for success. Checking the box of abstaining from alcohol is quite an achievement, but it is just the foundation for the bigger transformational work you are here to do.

In the final chapter of this book, I'll offer you my closing thoughts on and encouragement for staying the course in your new relationship (or lack thereof) with alcohol and using the momentum you've gained to step boldly into your truest potential.

CHAPTER 12

Unbottled Potential

Breaking Through to Your Best Life

Sobriety itself is today's high, for it is ultimately
in the most centered consciousness that we find
our power to transcend the world.

Marianne Williamson, *Illuminata*

You've probably caught on by now that this is not a book about changing your relationship with alcohol so that you can drink differently. This is a book about changing your relationship with alcohol so that you have the space to create a life so beautiful that alcohol becomes entirely insignificant to you. This is my hope for you.

In fact, it is not only my *hope* for you but also my mission and purpose to awaken you to your potential through the path of elective sobriety. This is not a path I chose intentionally; hardly. If you had told me a few years ago that I'd be a coach, speaker, and author who talked about spirituality, personal growth, and—excuse me—alcohol-free living, I would have laughed to hysterics. Yet I'm eternally grateful that it has led me here. It is my honor to do this work and share this important message with you.

It's difficult to believe that just a handful of years ago, I was a Party Girl, lost and without purpose and true confidence. I was a victim of my own circumstances, with barely enough self-awareness to believe I could profoundly shift the trajectory of my life. Over the course of just five years, I've watched my wildest dreams come true before my very eyes. Today, I live an alcohol-free life that is full of miracles. It is the life I spent years reading about in personal development books, wondering if it was all too good to be true. It wasn't. I've accomplished more in my short time as an alcohol-free woman than I did in over a decade of ex-hausting myself trying to keep up with the work-hard, play-hard lifestyle. Choosing to step out of the haze of the drinking culture allowed me to unbottle my potential in ways I could have never imagined. I've achieved the emotional grounding, wholehearted relationships, career fulfillment, financial abundance, and spiri-tual connection that I spent years yearning for.

I wake up most days feeling vibrant and inspired. My sense of self-worth is higher than ever before, and I feel confident and capable of handling anything the Universe throws my way. From unfettered joy and happiness to heartache and grief, I feel emotionally resilient and ready to show up for it all with ease and grace. I have a network of incredible friends and peers, and I feel more supported and connected than ever. Most im-portantly, I am happy. I am truly, deeply happy. This is the life I want for you.

The best part is that with alcohol out of the way, all of this has come to me with relative ease. Yes, I've put in hard work—I've cried, thrown temper tantrums, bitched, moaned, and wanted to give up more than once. I've veered off course more times than I can count. And yet, because of my commitment to relentlessly show up for myself, I've found ways to get back on course more quickly. Because of this commitment, I haven't had to burn myself out, compromise my morals, push and prod, or scheme to achieve the life of my dreams.

All of this is available to you. I have no specific advantage that has afforded me this life. I am here to clear a path and go a few steps before you to light the way. I am here to offer you my hand and my voice in the reassurance that you, too, are meant to live the most wild and wonderful version of your life that you can imagine. In fact, I believe that your biggest dream is not only possible, but also a mere fraction of what you are capable of achieving if you choose to follow the principles I've shared to help you break up with alcohol and break through to your best life.

As you embark on this journey, it's imperative that you remember the importance of both holding the vision *and* doing the work. This is the potent combination that will guide you away from the ordinary and into the extraordinary. There is no shortcut, quick fix, or magical weekend retreat that will change the trajectory of your life. Likewise, there is no number of self-help books you can read, inspirational accounts you can follow, or accountability groups you can join that will transform how you show up in this world. *You* are the only one who can shift your reality.

Don't get me wrong; these tools can absolutely help you as you endeavor to step into your best life—and I hope this book is helping you on your way—but you are the only one who has authority over changing your behaviors, and that starts with shifting your mindset and your priorities. If you are willing to commit to unlearning the romanticized viewpoints you have about alcohol and pursuing potential above all else, I trust that you will go far.

If you follow the methods outlined in this book, you'll have what you need to rewire your mindset and slowly shift your relationship with alcohol. This will clear the way for you to begin stepping into your truest potential in every aspect of your life.

It is very possible that you'll face recurring resistance and temptation, urging you to deny your potential and revert to your old ways or persuading you that you can have the best of both worlds. You may lose sight of your potential and be lured to reach for the temporary comfort of a cocktail. In these moments, remember why you started. This journey isn't about deprivation or moral righteousness. You are not making a choice to change your relationship with alcohol because you are bad or wrong or because you *can't* drink. You are making this decision to remove alcohol from your life because you know that you are meant for something extraordinary, and alcohol is doing nothing but getting in the way.

In my coaching practice, I've been fortunate enough to support many individuals, just like you, who have a bigger vision for what their lives could look like with alcohol out of the picture.

I want you to share the experience of my clients Fiona and Erin, who have reimagined their social lives and found new, exciting ways to have fun in sobriety.

I want you to follow in the footsteps of my clients Danielle and Cori and make friends with your emotions, learning to communicate and express feelings ranging from sadness and grief to joy and elation.

I want you to reimagine your friendships and experience the fulfillment of attracting new, high-vibe connections into your life, just like my clients Kara and Kristen.

I want you to experience the joys of sober dating like my clients Nina and Bethany or strengthen your current relationships just as my clients Shannon and Naomi have.

Finally, what I most want for you is to live more authentically, find your calling, and discover an unwavering connection with the Universe like my clients Maria and Tessa.

This is the life I want for you; this is the life that is available to you now. I believe that you have so much more to offer than you can achieve with alcohol in the picture. My purpose as a teacher and writer is to remind you of your light, your magnificence, and the infinite potential that resides within you, just waiting to be unbottled and shared with the world.

This journey isn't for everyone. Yet I believe you have found your way to this book for a reason. I believe you know on some instinctual level that you are meant for and capable of unbelievable things in this lifetime. If there is an area in your life where you feel dissatisfied, stuck, or downright unhappy, taking a break from alcohol will bring you clarity and freedom.

What's more, I believe that now, more than ever before, we need conscious individuals who are willing to show up fully, do the work, and embrace the truest expression of their potential available to them. I do not believe that potential can be properly expressed if you are actively spending time and energy diluting yourself with alcohol.

Whether you're sober curious or already alcohol-free, you are part of a bold, brave new group of leaders that I believe has the capacity to impact this world in marvelous ways. As you step into your unbottled life, I'd like to leave you with some final steps for embracing all this journey has to offer:

Step 1: **Accept the assignment.** You are here for a reason. Your Inner Guide would not have gifted you with sober curiosity if this were not a path you were intended to explore. With this curiosity, you have been given an assignment. At first, you might view this assignment begrudgingly with a Why me? point of view. You might not understand why all your friends get to go on living their carefree, boozy lives, and *you* have to be the one feeling weird about alcohol.

I choose to believe your sober curiosity is not some cruel punishment from the Universe but rather a divine assignment. You have been called to step up to your potential in a way that isn't available to you as a drinker. This is no punishment. Instead, it's a phenomenal opportunity. If you allow yourself to view sobriety in this way, suddenly, being alcohol-free will feel like an elite secret club you've been given the password for. There will be many times when you'll be tempted to decide the assignment is over. In these moments, I invite you to have full trust in your Inner Guide and know that you were not guided to this path at random. Your call to elective sobriety is a miraculous assignment; I encourage you to accept it with fervor.

Step 2: **Practice patience.** Patience is crucial when recalibrating for a new normal. Try your best to release any expectations about results or timelines, and trust that everything is happening with perfect timing. It will seem that some aspects of your life are temporarily more difficult. In these times, it is important to remind yourself that things aren't getting worse; they're getting real. You are acclimating to a reality you've been hiding from for years as a drinker. You are no different from a toddler learning to walk. Life will feel wobbly and off-balance in some areas, but rest assured you've got what it takes to stand tall and steady. You are not incapable; you're just inexperienced. Practice patience with yourself and with the process. There is no timeline. Wherever you are now is perfect.

Step 3: **Embrace your place on the cutting edge.** Congratulations! Your decision to explore an alcohol-free lifestyle has officially landed you on the cutting edge of . . . well, everything. Elective sobriety is a rather new concept, so you may often feel ahead of your time. I encourage you to stay the course. You are on the cusp of a breakthrough that will change your life and the lives of many others. Yet being on the cutting edge will require you to practice humility and patience; this is a leadership position. Your responsibility as a leader is to be a gracious teacher to others in order to keep the elective sobriety movement in good standing. Remember: You are not here to preach to others but to be an example. Put intention into demonstrating how robust an alcohol-free lifestyle can be. Be generous in the presence of willing students or other individuals curious about sobriety. Likewise, be gentle in the presence of those who seem uninterested or unimpressed.

It is not your job to convert anyone to your way of seeing and experiencing the world. The best you can do is demonstrate what it's like to experience the benefits of sobriety and kindly answer questions when asked. Your demonstration has the power to shift how others view the experience of sobriety in profound ways. You are part of a movement that is positioning sobriety as a bold choice rather than an ill-fated consequence. I'm so proud of you.

Step 4: **Celebrate your magnificence.** You will experience so many firsts as an alcohol-free person. Commit to celebrating your magnificence and honoring your commitment to this process. In my life, the most difficult moments I had to face head-on—with no alcohol to numb the experience—have been my proudest moments. From sober events to tough conversations to overwhelming emotions like joy and heartache, I have made an important practice of celebrating the pure, raw fullness of life.

Step 5: **Unbottle your potential.** With alcohol no longer in your way, the inner voice of fear may still attempt to keep you stuck. You may be persuaded to avoid your emotions, stay complacent in your relationships, play small in your career, or avoid tapping into your authenticity or connecting with Spirit. In those moments, remember that you are always being guided. Your Inner Guide is a seasoned shepherd and would not lead you astray. If you have a calm sense that you are not living up to your potential in any area of your life, view this as a certain opportunity to grow and self-express. Know that your Inner Guide will show you the resources and teachers you need to support you on this journey. I hope this book has been one such resource, and I would be honored to continue as your teacher.

It would be my greatest joy to have you step out of the social construct of the drinking culture and step into your magnificence. My triumph is your embodiment of your potential. We need you awake. We need whatever it is you have to offer the world. We need you to show up emotionally, bravely choosing to feel all the feels. We need you showing up in your relationships—platonic, romantic, and beyond—as an example of how to truly express your potential purpose. You have the capacity within you to be absolutely magnificent, fully embodied, deeply connected, authentically expressed, and wholly supported. This is your invitation to claim what was meant for you, to raise your energetic frequency, and to unbottle *your* potential.

Resources

On the following pages, you'll find a list of resources, including books, podcasts, articles, and more, that have supported me in un-bottling my own potential. These are resources I return to over and over (yes, I've read or listened to most of these books multiple times!). *I'll also keep an updated digital version of this list on my website, amandakuda.com/unbottledresources.*

BOOKS

Alcohol-Free Living

Alcohol Explained: Understand Why You Drink and How to Stop by William Porter

Euphoric: Ditch Alcohol and Gain a Happier, More Confident You by Karolina Rzadkowolska

Not Drinking Tonight: A Guide to Creating a Sober Life You Love by Amanda White

Quit Like a Woman: The Radical Choice to Not Drink in a Culture Obsessed with Alcohol by Holly Whitaker

Sober Curious: The Blissful Sleep, Greater Focus, Limitless Presence, and Deep Connection Awaiting Us All on the Other Side of Alcohol by Ruby Warrington

The Sober Girl Society Handbook: Why Drinking Less Means Living More by Millie Gooch

This Naked Mind: Control Alcohol, Find Freedom, Discover Happiness & Change Your Life by Annie Grace

Spirituality

Light Is the New Black: A Guide to Answering Your Soul's Calling and Working Your Light by Rebecca Campbell

The Power of Intention: Learning to Co-create Your World Your Way by Wayne W. Dyer

A Return to Love: Reflections on the Principles of "A Course in Miracles" by Marianne Williamson

Spirit Junkie: A Radical Road to Self-Love and Miracles by Gabrielle Bernstein

Sex and Relationships

Come as You Are: The Surprising New Science That Will Transform Your Sex Life by Emily Nagoski

Conscious Loving: The Journey to Co-commitment by Gay Hendricks and Kathlyn Hendricks

Pussy: A Reclamation by Regena Thomashauer

Personal Growth and Self-Optimization

Atomic Habits: An Easy & Proven Way to Build Good Habits & Break Bad Ones by James Clear

The Big Leap: Conquer Your Hidden Fear and Take Life to the Next Level by Gay Hendricks

The Dark Side of the Light Chasers: Reclaiming Your Power, Creativity, Brilliance, and Dreams by Debbie Ford

The Gifts of Imperfection: Let Go of Who You Think You're Supposed to Be and Embrace Who You Are by Brené Brown

The Six Pillars of Self-Esteem by Nathaniel Branden

PODCASTS

Alcohol-Free Living

Euphoric the Podcast

Hello Someday

Recovery Rocks

Seltzer Squad

Sober Curious

A Sober Girls Guide

Take a Break from Drinking

Unbottled Potential

Spirituality, Personal Growth, and Self-Optimization

Almost 30

Expanded

Good Life Project

Highest Self Podcast

The Life Stylist

Mark Groves Podcast

SimplyBe.

Episodes

Huberman Lab: "What Alcohol Does to Your Body, Brain & Health"—hubermanlab.com/what-alcohol-does-to-your-body-brain-health

This Podcast Will Kill You: "Alcohol: Beer for Thought"—
thispodcastwillkillyou.com/2021/11/02/episode-85-alcohol-beer
-for-thought

ARTICLES AND OTHER RESOURCES

"Back by Popular Demand: Are You an Abstainer or a
Moderator?" by Gretchen Rubin—gretchenrubin.com/articles
/abstainer-vs-moderator

Calm meditation app—calm.com

Create the Love Cards game—createthelove.com/cards

Havening Techniques—havening.org

Headspace meditation app—headspace.com

Insight Timer meditation app—insighttimer.com

Where Should We Begin?—A Game of Stories card game—
game.estherperel.com

Acknowledgments

I had no idea what a growth journey writing a book would be. I have tremendous gratitude for the many angels—of this earth and beyond—who supported me through this massive initiation.

To begin, I owe so much to my talented book proposal coach, Richelle Fredson. Richelle, thank you for helping me craft my dream into what I can humbly say was a book proposal masterpiece. I'm grateful for your expertise, tutelage, voice note counseling, and cheerleading. I am your biggest fan, and I honestly can't shut up about you.

I have tremendous gratitude for my (dream) literary agents, Steve Troha and Jan Baumer of Folio Literary Management. Thank you for seeing my vision for the world and for helping me find the perfect publishing home to share that vision. Thank you for holding my hand as I navigated the adventure of becoming a first-time author and for being my advocates on this journey. You made the process so easy I quite literally forgot about it (but that's a story for another book).

Thank you to the team at Avery and Penguin Random House for trusting me to create this book. I'm eternally grateful to Lucia Watson for seeing the need for this book and excitedly signing on to support me in writing it. Thank you for your patience as I turned in multiple shitty first drafts and found my voice as an author. Thank you also to my editor, Suzy Swartz, for your genius in editing this project; I appreciate your support, guidance, and attention to detail. Thank you, also, to the many hands at

Avery who touched this book or supported me in unknown ways throughout this process. You all made my childhood dreams come true.

I would not be who I am or where I am without my family and greatest life assignments. Thank you for always loving me.

To my mother, Nadine: Thank you for moving mountains to support my dreams. You nourished my kindness and creativity; I'm not sure how you did it all. You were a model of hard work and compassion, and I am grateful for your love.

To my father, Mike: Thank you for always being on call to help me figure it out and for encouraging my determination and curiosity. You always seem to pull off the impossible and have—for better or worse—helped me believe I can do the same.

To my brother, Brian: Being your sister has taught me so much. Thank you for being my first student (willing or not).

To my bonus family—Dallis, Brandon, Melissa, Harper, and Ella: Thank you for including me and always supporting me; I'm so lucky to have you all in my life. Dallis, you influenced and supported me so generously when I most needed it. I can't thank you enough.

To my fur family: Sweet Monroe, to whom this book is dedicated. You brought me twelve years of pure love and joy. I'm grateful to have spent four of those years fully present and awake to your love. I believe that your departure was divine and created the necessary space for me to birth this book into the world. And little Martini, my ironically named Yorki-poo, I'm grateful you're now the only martini in my life.

To my soul family who have supported me during this entire process and beyond: Kate, Kristin, Rose Ann, Jennifer, Carly, Upasna, Britni, Tim, Courtney, Heather, and Vasavi—you each inspire me in profound ways. I honestly don't know where I would be without the unique magic you each bring into my life.

To my Spiritual Writers, you helped me rekindle my passion for writing and created a safe space for me to share my soul. I cherish our monthly writing circles and weekends writing in the woods. You've helped me find my confidence and know myself in a different way.

I'm also grateful for my family at Athletic Outcomes, who keep me strong and probably do more than they know to keep me sane. I couldn't have picked a better home away from home.

To the mentors and coaches who have guided me along the journey of becoming an entrepreneur and author: Kerissa Kuis, Kim Argetsinger, Jolene Park, Taylor Nations, Annie Lalla, Eben Pagan, Anand Rao, Jessica Zweig, Megan Taylor, and Amanda Merit—I have grown further, faster with your support and encouragement. Thank you for seeing my light and encouraging me to shine bright.

Many teachers have contributed to my transformation, some of whom may never know the tremendous impact they've had on my life: the late Wayne Dyer, Rebecca Campbell, Brené Brown, and so many more. It's miraculous how far you can get with a Google search bar, a podcast app, and an audiobook subscription.

A special thanks to Marianne Williamson and Gabrielle Bernstein: I am endlessly inspired by your work and your presence on this planet. Your work as spiritual teachers guided me to find my own path of service and spiritual devotion. I am beyond grateful for the work that you do.

I am also forever indebted to the brave women who paved the way in the early days of the sobriety and alcohol-free movements: Annie Grace, Holly Whitaker, Laura McKowen, and Ruby Warrington, in particular—your work has created a new path for many, including me. Thank you for speaking loudly—I know it wasn't easy. To my other sober friends and alcohol-free crusaders, I love you all so much and am so proud of the impact we are having on the world. Much love to Karolina Rzadkowolska and Jen Kautsch for being my running buddies in the alcohol-free movement. Thank you, especially, to Tawny Lara for being the best sober sexpert and book-writing buddy a gal could have.

Thank you to my dear friends who helped me fulfill the quintessential writer's dream of holing up in a quaint, quiet place to birth their creations into the world. I was blessed to have three opportunities to do so. To my soul sister, Melissa Abdine, for sharing your dreamy cottage—your healing home was just what I needed. To Mason and Christina Ayer for allowing me to experience your cozy cabin in the snow-covered mountains—it was a writer's dream. To Andie Roeder for your hospitality at Club Marina, Costa Rica—the Nosara magic is what brought this book home.

Massive love to my clients and students, who have helped shape who I am as a coach, teacher, and writer. You inspire me daily with your tenacity, curiosity, and commitment. I'm so honored to support you.

Though I've inevitably left someone out, please know that if our paths have crossed, I believe wholeheartedly that it is for a reason. I am grateful for you.

Finally, thank you to *you*, my reader. Exploring a book like this requires bravery. I know you are a visionary and that you are—without question—meant to do amazing things in this world. Your potential is what inspires me the most. It is my joy and honor to support, encourage, and inspire you to step into your greatness.